ALSO FROM QUIPPERY

And more books on the way

SEEDS & WEEDS

THE FUNNIEST THINGS PEOPLE HAVE SAID ABOUT

GARDENING

Created by
Craig and Erich Pearson

A *Quippery* BOOK
The Funniest Things People Have Said

Quippery LLC
Fairfield, Iowa 52557 USA

ISBN: 978-1-949571-05-9

Published in the United States by Quippery LLC

Cover design by George Foster (fostercovers.com) and Erich Pearson

Printed with chlorine-free ink, on acid-free paper supplied by a Forest Stewardship Council certified supplier.

quippery.com

SEEDS & WEEDS

TABLE OF CONTENTS

By all means, read this book aloud at garden parties. But be cautioned to wait until guests have finished eating. You don't want their laughter to cause them to shoot garden salad from their nostrils.

— Miss Nanners

IS GARDENING FOR YOU?

One in three American households is now growing food in home and community gardens. Is gardening for you?

- Do you relish being outside, communing with the wonder of life, the miracle of growth, the spirit of Mother Nature?
- Do you fancy the color green?
- Do you enjoy bending over and looking down?
- For protracted periods?
- Do you enjoy getting "down and dirty"?
- Including dirt under your fingernails?
- How well do you tolerate mosquito, chigger, and tick bites?
- Do you enjoy the primordial satisfaction of harvesting vegetables you've grown yourself, in intimate partnership with nature, then savoring the ultimate locally grown and freshly harvested food?

- Even when you see a slug emerging from your salad and motoring across your dinner plate?
- Are you attracted to the possibility that for as little as 500 hours of your time you can reduce your food costs by as much as $100?
- Will you be OK paying the equivalent of $64 for a tomato?
- And that tomato being maybe not quite as perfect as you can buy in the store?
- But warmed by the sun in your own garden?
- Do you enjoy repetitive activities? Like pulling the same weeds out of the same spots every day?
- Are you generally comfortable with compost?
- Do you comprehend that soil is more than just dirt? That soil is, like, *everything*?
- Is your soil friable? Or even pliable? Will you pledge to make it viable, reliable, *undeniable?* Will you promise to befriend it, tend it, and amend it? Will you commit to venerating and *regenerating* it?

- When you turn over a spadeful of soil and see a bright, plump brown earthworm, do you feel a warm sense of camaraderie and partnership?
- How about when you discover you've inadvertently — *Oops!* So sorry, little guy! — sliced it in two?
- When you get together with other gardeners, will you be able to hold your own discussing the pros and cons of annuals, perennials, and millennials?
- How well do you endure back pain?

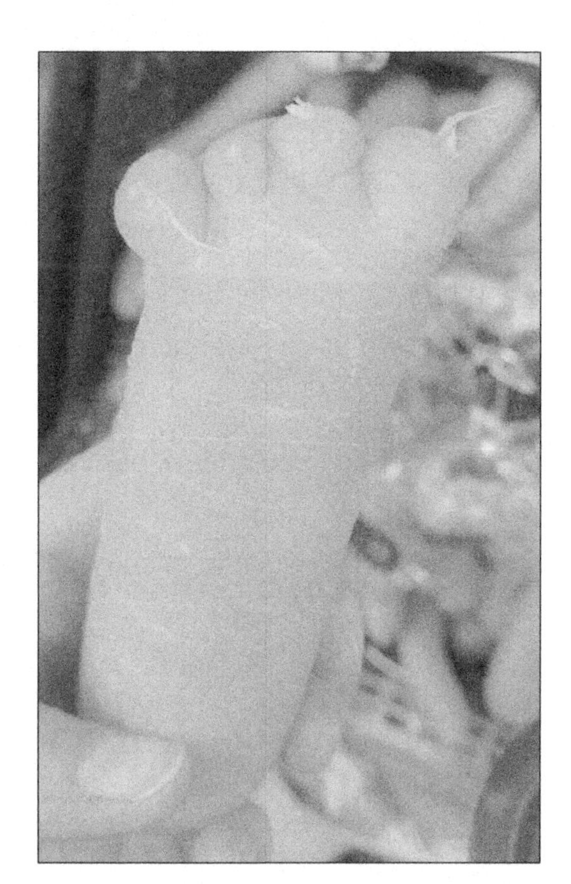

- Will you feel your relationship with your raspberry bushes is one-sided if after spending three years lovingly tending to them, weeding and watering, and, in return, your bushes have yielded a total harvest of just four lentil-sized berries?
- How would you feel having a magnificent, 20-foot-tall pear tree in your front yard, producing bushels of plump pears every season?
- And for some unknown reason, these pears never ripen but remain rock hard.
- How about an apple tree, which you purchase as a sapling from a professional grower with an agronomy PhD, who says this is his favorite variety, it produces abundant and delicious applies, and it grows well in your area?
- And your actual tree produces small, hard, often misshapen, wincingly tart apples — apples that are nevertheless attractive to bees, who

burrow into them — and then, after six or seven years, the tree gradually withers and dies and you have to have it removed?

- How will you feel when you go out to your garden expecting to spend a few minutes harvesting some herbs — and discover your garden has become a *racoon latrine*, the feces necessitating removal with the same painstaking care that an elite, highly-trained squad of professionals gives to removing hazardous waste or a live bomb?
- Are you on generally good terms with your lawn?
- Even when it's freely welcoming every species of crabgrass and weed?
- And when, driven by some invisible, invincible force, it relentlessly overtakes your garden, to the point where your options are to rototill your garden and start over or move elsewhere?
- Do you feel that rabbits are an integral part of nature and deserve to have their natural needs met, just like every other living thing?

- Even when they've somehow managed to penetrate the impenetrable fencing you've placed around your Korean lilacs before the frigid winter, with rabbit pellets evenly distributed on both sides of the fencing as if the fence did not exist, with no breach in the fencing and no burrowing beneath it, and with rabbits having thoroughly stripped the bark from the lower branches, leaving the now naked branches gleaming like bones in the sunlight and your lilacs surely doomed?
- When you see deer, do marvel at this mythical marvel of grace?
- Even when they've levitated over your fence into your yard and are nonchalantly munching on your apples?
- Are you aware that being an effective gardener requires a level of knowledge and training equal to becoming a medical doctor?
- Which means knowledge of botany, agronomy, biology, meteorology, philology, chemistry, and alchemy?
- And *Latin*?
- As for biology — You don't want to suffer ridicule for ignorance of the lodicule. Or be stigmatized for ignorance of the stigma. And when people ask you questions about anthers — you'd better have anthers.
- And what about the biological reproductive issues? Do you identify more with the pistil or the stamen? Or perhaps you identify as a trans plant?

- Chemistry — Will you be comfortable with learning soil chemistry? Basic knowledge like whether your soil is too "basic?" The macronutrients and micronutrients every plant needs to survive and where to get them in easy-to-swallow capsule or tablet form? Will you enjoy learning how to test your soil, including determining whether multiple-choice, short-answer, or essay questions are best? And speaking of chemistry, do you know where you'll go to get a good lab coat, test tubes, and eye protectors?

- And even though you've always wondered why anyone would study Latin, a long-dead language that even ancient Romans hated learning, are you prepared to learn the essential Latin terminology you'll need as a gardener? Should you shelter your children from *Phaseolus vulgaris*? Are you sure you'll want to touch a *Phaseolus coccineus*? Do you even want to think about *Helianthus annuus*?

- Do you have the Navy Seal-level fortitude to withstand the insanity-inducing itch-cream-taunting itchiness resulting from wild parsnip rash — your descent into madness compounded by not finding wild parsnip anywhere in your garden or yard?
- Will it bother you to see your plants openly and shamelessly having sex, in broad daylight, in front of you and all the other plants?
- Without protection?
- And often with themselves?
- Does pondering this make you think about the Sex Pistils?

- Will you look forward strolling out to your garden to enjoy a tranquil afternoon break from the pressures of work, a languid break in the warm summer sun, songbirds chirruping, breezes flowing around you, allowing yourself some well-deserved **BAM! BAM!** industrial air power staples shoot into the back of each hand straight through your brand-new protective garden gloves **BAM!** a power staple to the back of your knee **BAM!** another power staple to the identical spot on your left hand. Three menacing furry objects the size of golf balls zero in around your head. You sprint like mad away from the garden, your whole body aching. Now you circle around to the other side to view the garden and from 30 feet away see three dozen heavily muscled Blackwater-trained black and yellow bumblebee mercenary assassins swirling in a cloud above the ground where you'd unsuspectingly bent down to pull stray grass, each of them a miniature SuperCobra attack helicopter having constructed a stealth attack base just below ground the night before. And oh your hands the pain won't be going away for weeks and now that they've shown you what they can do you're awaiting their demand for ten percent off the top of your weekly household income plus assorted daily table scraps in return for protection. . . .

- Will you be able to maintain equanimity if everything you have labored long and hard to grow is killed by frost, deer, hail, locusts, moles, rabbits, aphids, asparagus beetles, cabbage worms, carrot rust flies, Colorado potato beetles, cucumber beetles, cutworms, flea beetles, leaf miners, Mexican bean beetles, slugs, snails, squash bugs, squash vine borers, tomato hornworms, whiteflies, cabbage maggots, caterpillars, tarnished plant bugs, Japanese beetles, scales, jealous neighborhood gardeners who would rather destroy others' gardens than suffer gardens superior to their own, mindless texting motorists who drive off the road and bulldoze across your yard and garden, a random sinkhole opening beneath your property and instantly swallowing your garden and house and yard and maybe your neighborhood in one gulp . . . or some combination of the above?

If you're OK with all this, then gardening just might be for you.

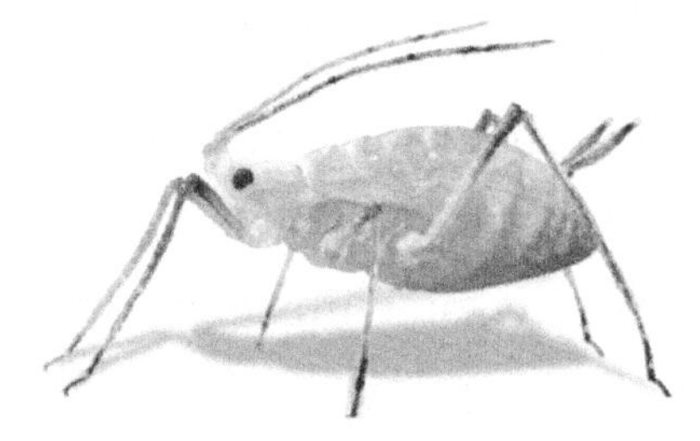

"If garden beginners knew in advance all the troubles in their way, they might never begin."
— Leonard Robbins
Kind of like having kids!

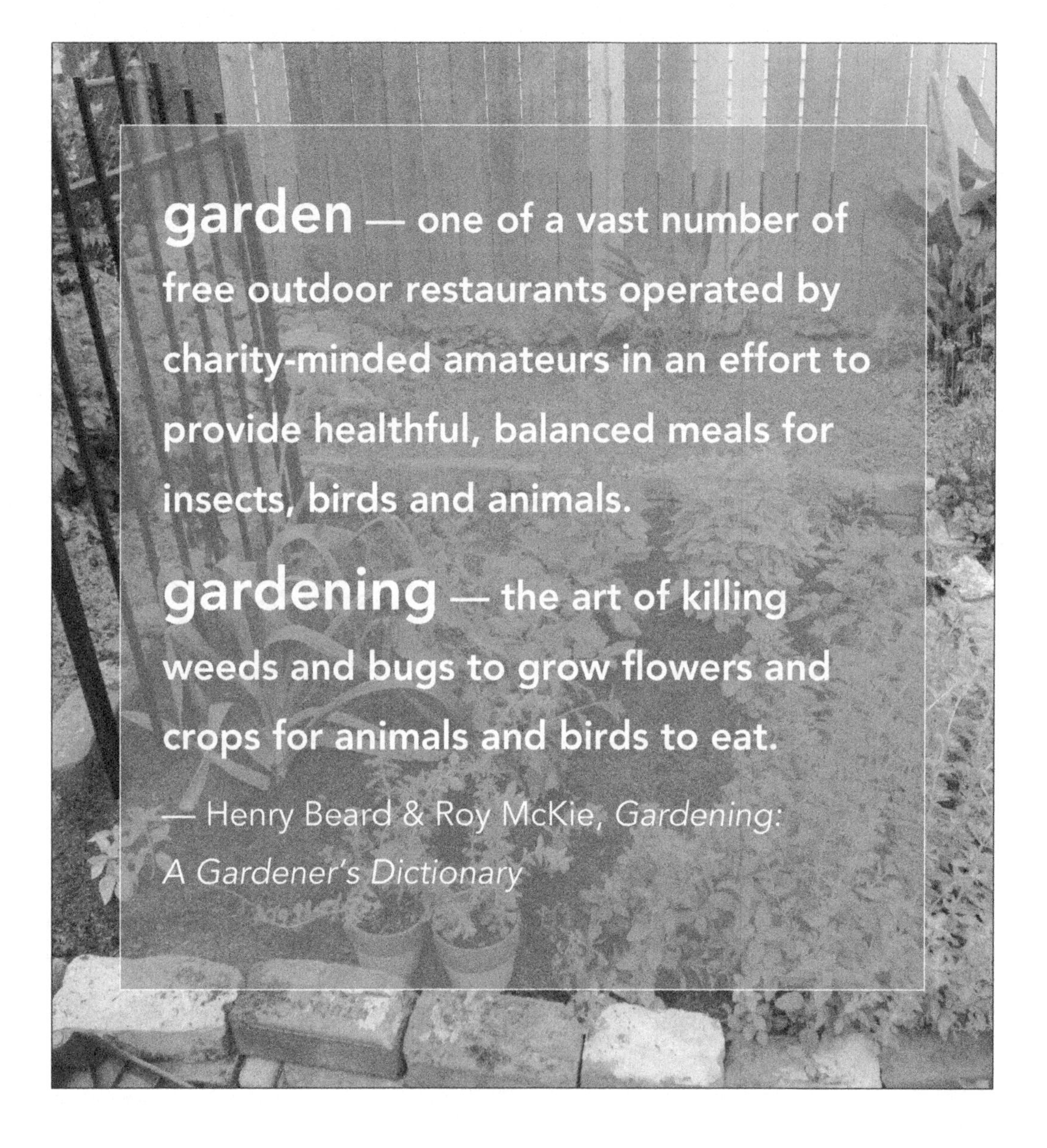

garden — one of a vast number of free outdoor restaurants operated by charity-minded amateurs in an effort to provide healthful, balanced meals for insects, birds and animals.

gardening — the art of killing weeds and bugs to grow flowers and crops for animals and birds to eat.

— Henry Beard & Roy McKie, *Gardening: A Gardener's Dictionary*

GETTING STARTED

from The Onion

Tips For Growing Your Own Vegetable Garden

- Before you start planting, make sure your local terrain is conducive to growing the kinds of vegetables you can stuff with cheese and deep-fry.
- After supplying your plants with soil and water, sprinkle a few gummy bears on top as a little treat.
- To prevent your plants from becoming waterlogged, be sure to regularly curse or otherwise offend the Mayan rain god Tohil.
- Earthworms are extremely beneficial for cultivating soil, and you can legally pay them next to nothing!
- Tomatoes can be vine-ripened for several days in your home before being hurled at people you disagree with.

WHAT GIVES PEOPLE FEELINGS OF POWER

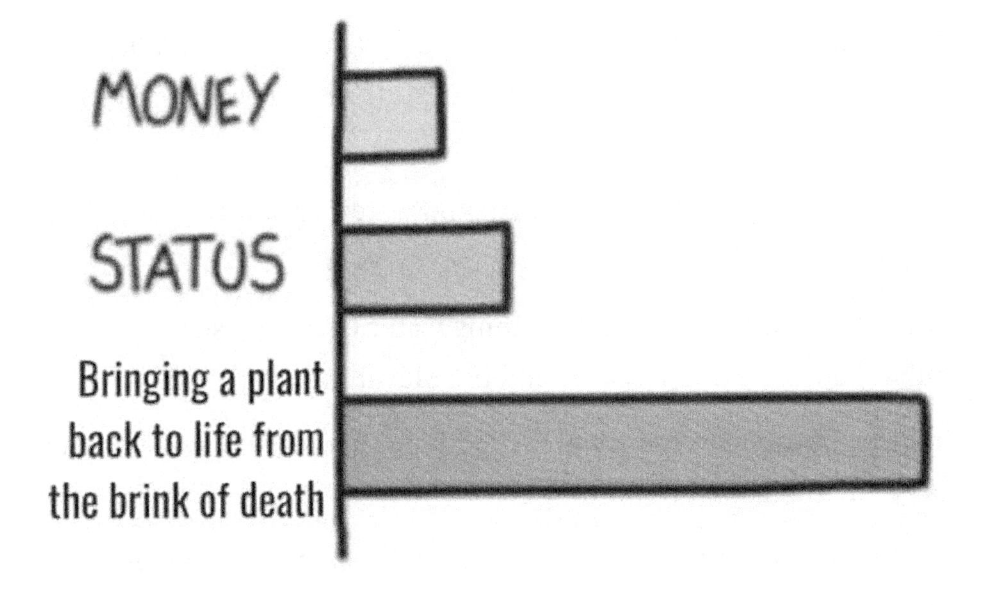

TOOLS OF THE TIRADE

Gardening requires tools. Yes, you can probably get by using only your hands, but why? Here's a brief guide to the tools you'll need.

The dibber

The dibber is the first tool you should get.

As you see in the illustration, you push the dibber into the warm, moist, fertile earth, then withdraw it and insert your seed into the hole. Then you repeat the process for as many seeds as you're up for planting.

Lubrication should not be needed even if the soil is dry and brittle.

The dibber also goes by other names, including *dibble* and *dibbler*. Some people mistakenly call it a *dribbler*, but this is not correct.

As simple as this tool looks, there are many varieties to choose from.

There's the *straight dibber*, the *T-handled dibber*, and the *L-shaped dibber* (handle only on one side). An enterprising gardener invented the *trowel dibber*, with a trowel on one side, dibber on the other.

Once that first dual-use dibber device emerged, it was inevitable that others would follow. Next came the *marching baton dibber*, the *umbrella dibber,* and the *Olympic torch dibber.* A *TV remote dibber* is expected soon.

Then the competition in the dibber space exploded. Angel investors swarmed the country, hither and thither, unditheringly ready to deliver millions to any daft dibber idea.

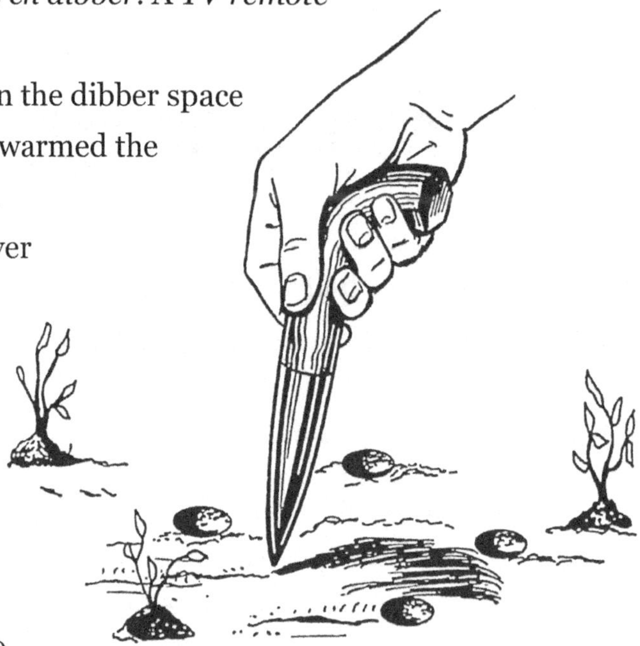

Some companies rebranded the dibber. First came the *Doober*™ and then the *Deeber*™. (The name *Dweeber* remains available). Both Doobers and Deebers came in garden-themed colors — raspberry red, kale green, pumpkin orange, and elegant eggplant black.

Then *Dilbert* comic strip artist Scott Adams and his merchandisers, sensing a chance to expand beyond Dilbert t-shirts, mugs, neckties, and toilet augers, brought the *Dilbert Dibber* to market with great fanfare.

But none of these were true innovations. Even Dilbert's international name recognition proved no match for the aggressive dibble innovator who grabbed yards of garden center shelf space when she created the *fast-*

acting dibber, the *extra strength dibber*, the *low-fat dibber*, and the *unscented dibber*. Currently in development: the *cheese crust dibber*.

But just as she was about to commandeer the dibber market, some enterprising Stanford students, working in their dorm rooms, developed an app that connected dibber users worldwide *through their dibbers*. Successive upgrades enabled gardeners to test their soil . . . test their pregnancy status . . . even test whether it's raining and signal gardeners to go inside.

With each new development, giddy gardeners gathered in groups outside garden centers for days ahead of the release. Even non-gardeners lined up to acquire them.

But then came the game-changer. The definitive dibber disrupter.

A ninth-grade girl in Del Rio, Texas, for her science project, developed a fully digital, fully self-dibbering dibber. Every comfort and safety feature had been seamlessly integrated, even enabling gardeners to start their dibbers remotely, so they were warmed up by the time they got to their gardens. Hers was a concept no one had ever conceptualized.

And the future? Rumors swirl about self-elongating dibbers that turn into Harry Potter-esque Elder wands, with who knows what powers. And further elongating dibbers that can be ridden, broomstick-like, anywhere one pleases. With the current pace of progress, who's to say what's possible and what's not?

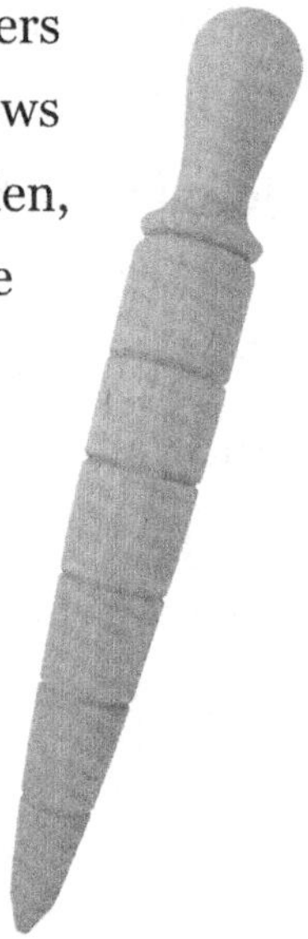

But no matter how upstart the upgrades, no matter how quantum the leaps, basic design principles have remained in place.

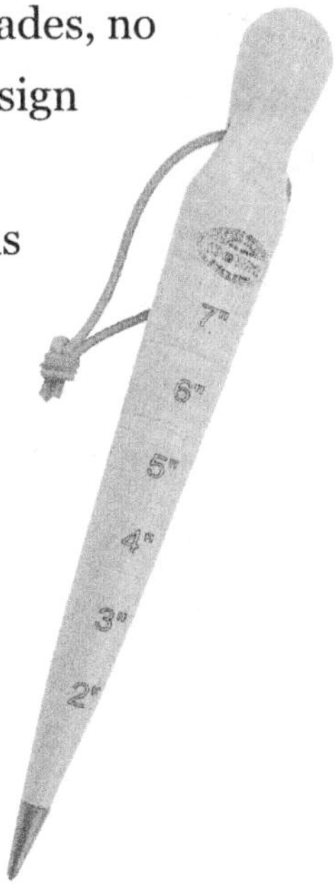

Because when it comes to dibbers, as with certain other good things in life, size doesn't matter. You mainly want your dibber to feel comfortable in your hand — solid, smooth to the touch, pleasing to grip, and with good heft, delivering the same simple earthy pleasures dibbers have always delivered.

A simple aid for a sacred act.

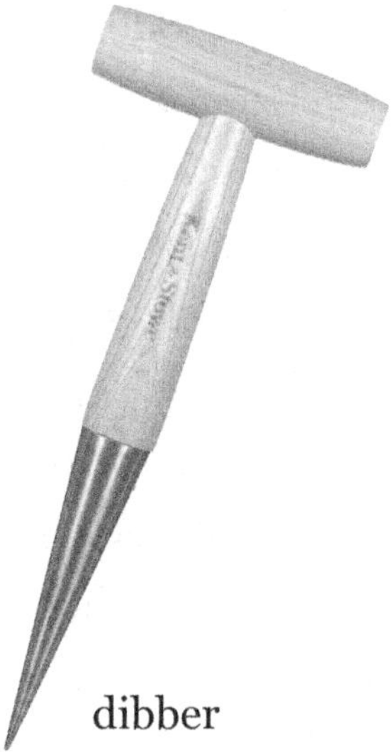

Dibber safety tip — Though most gardeners like to keep their dibbers handy, avoid carrying your dibber in your pocket unless you have a protective case for it. You don't want to accidentally dibber yourself.

Quippery
I'm a
GARDENER
Ask me about my
DIBBER
Quippery

The trowel

We won't repeat the worn-out lines that *gardening is learned by trowel and error* and *don't throw in the trowel.* We'll say them just this once and expect you'll remember them.

The trowel is a starter shovel. It's the shovel you give to four-year-olds who are just starting out in the garden. It's a teeny tiny shovel used for digging teeny tiny holes in the ground.

Be careful though. The trowel is a gateway tool, the beginning of a slippery slope. Once people start using trowels, it's only a matter of time before they go on to harder and more dangerous and addictive implements — shovels, backhoes, trenchers, and excavators.

Trowels themselves are wonderfully multi-purpose implements. Can't find anything to dish out the fruit salad or chili you're serving at your garden party? Just hose off your trowel off and you're good to go — it's the perfect size and shape. Your guests will admire your ingenuity.

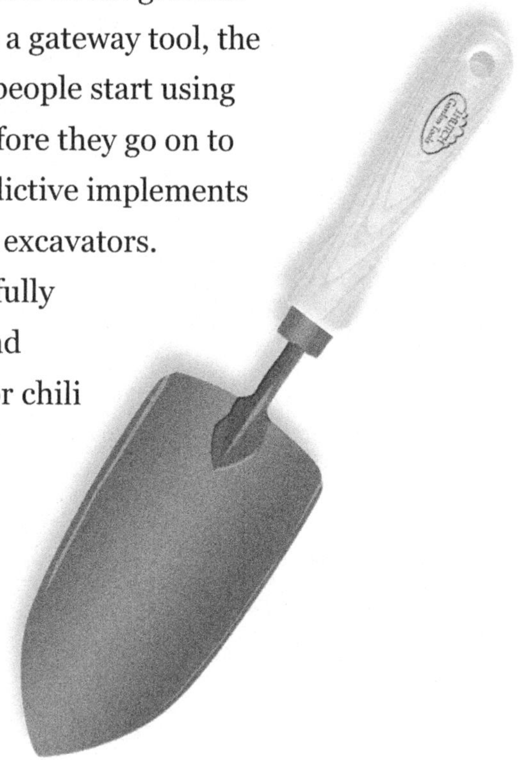

The shovel

The shovel was originally used for shoving things around on the ground so you didn't have to bend over all the time.

After a while folks realized it could also be used for digging holes in the ground — the original ground-breaking technology, you might say. This saved a lot of wear and tear on fingers and fingernails.

Digging holes was useful for many things, like burying stuff you don't want folks to see — treasure, bones, bodies, subways, etc.

Shovel safety tips —

- Shoveling is strenuous exercise, so do some warm-up exercises first — you don't want to start cold.
- Place the shovel in front of you.
- Put one foot on it.
- Slowly lean forward.
- When you're sure the shovel is "shovel ready," go ahead and hand it to the guy you've hired to do the work.

The mulch-making machine

This clever mechanism provides you with a reliable source of mulch to put around your flowers, vegetables, shrubs, and trees.

Oh, and it can also help you keep the weeds in your yard neatly trimmed, so that it looks like you have a decent lawn to anyone glancing down from private aircraft.

Mulch-making machine safety tip — Whatever you do, don't pick up this machine and use it to trim your hedges, even if there are a few of you to share the lifting. You don't want to end up in ER with a pulled muscle.

The hand mower

Some veteran gardeners are so in tune with plants that they can communicate with them — they're *plant whisperers*.

They generally don't let people know about their ability because they don't want to you to think they're crazy.

But they know what plants like and what they don't like.

One thing they *will* tell you: Plants *hate* the ear-splitting, root-stem-and-leaf-shuddering clamor of power mowers and weed whips. (They also hate low-flying jets, ambulance and police sirens, and highway noise.) Subjected to these noises, plants would pull themselves underground by the roots if they could.

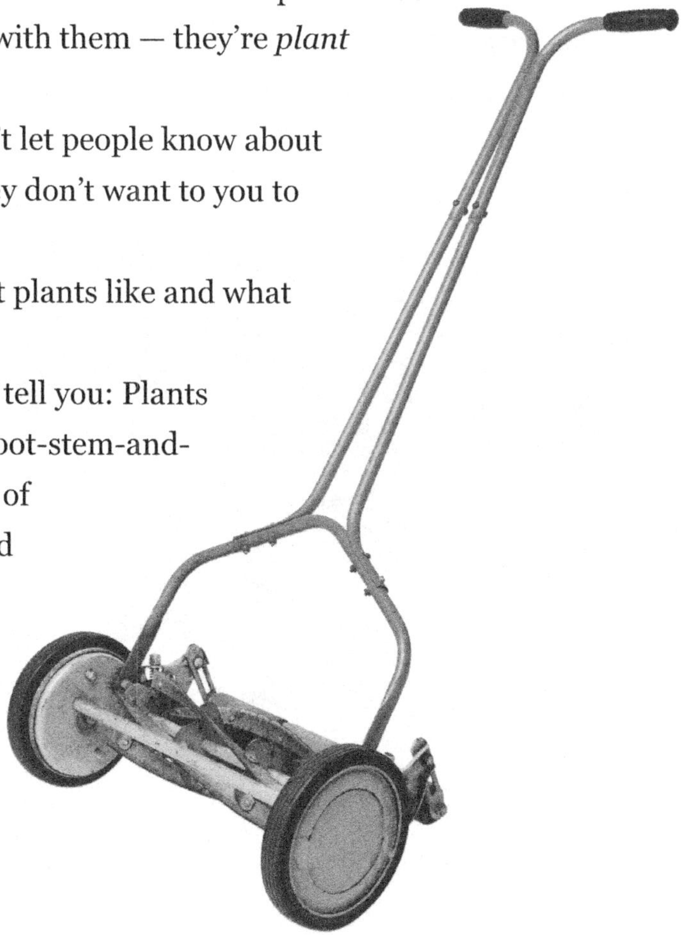

That's why plant whisperers use hand mowers.

The garden shed

Garden sheds are where you store your garden stuff. And a lot of other stuff. Garden sheds are where things go to die. They're black holes where, for a lot of things, when they go in, they never come out.

Which is exactly what makes sheds so cool. This is what gives them *character*.

AUTHENTIC SHED

Built by caring human hands with natural materials on-site near a real garden. Ages beautifully and greatly increases in value with the years.

Only clueless people wear brand shiny-new blue jeans.

Same with sheds. That's why premium shed makers will supply you with sheds already weathered and broken in, so that you'll look like the veteran, master gardener you aspire to be.

FAKE SHED

Built by machines in a windowless factory. Becomes increasingly dented and rusted, even more hideous than when new.

These remarkable sheds are fashioned of old wood, and everything inside is totally authentic. Starting with a collection of broken-in tools, of course, but also with everything else you'd expect in a good old shed.

Stacks of old seed catalogs and magazines. A cracked windowpane. A bike with flat tires and the chain hanging to the ground. A bike pump. A threadbare car tire. Lawn chairs with broken webbing. A red gasoline can. Spiderwebs and cobwebs and spiders. Layers of dust. A mound of sawdust. A mousetrap, unseen behind the magazine stacks, complete with desiccated dead mouse. An empty wasp nest fallen from the ceiling. The smell of last summer's gasoline spill. A couple of large, heavy, dusty bags of sphagnum moss, one of them split and leaking, dark sphagnum spreading ominously across the floor. Clay pots, some whole, some cracked, one in pieces. Empty egg cartons. Random pieces of ground cloth. A dusty box of CDs.

Making authentic, well worn-looking sheds has become an artform, and no two sheds are alike.

Normally it would take years to get your shed in such fine condition. That's why these sheds go for top dollar. They're assembled and furnished by hand, in small quantities, for the most discerning gardeners.

Who buys these lovingly curated sheds? Rich Middle Eastern sheikhs. That's right. They're the top customers. In the gardens outside their gold-gilded palaces, they want genuine American garden sheds — the premier Americana artifact, in their view — and they'll pay any price. They don't want them bigger than they'd be in America. But they must be authentic. Then they're flown on private jets to Saudi Arabia and Qatar and Oman.

The small, family-owned businesses that make these sheds for Middle Eastern royalty call them *sheikh shacks*.

Is there anything so garish and out-of-place-looking than a bright metal shed? Would you want your *house* to look like that? Your *dog's* house?

What do garden plants think about them? Let's get some quick reactions:

EGGPLANT – Egregious!

GARLIC – Garish!

ONIONS – Ungodly!

TULIPS – Too much!

BEGONIAS – Begone!

ASTERS – Asinine!

MORNING GLORIES – Moronic!

DILL – Dull!

POINSETTIAS – Pointless!

FORGET-ME-NOTS – Forget it!

RADISHES – Radiculous!

If you need five tools to solve a problem in the garden, four of them will be easy to find.

— Unknown

Your first job is to prepare the soil. The best tool for this is your neighbor's motorized garden tiller. If your neighbor does not own a garden tiller, suggest that he buy one.

— Dave Barry

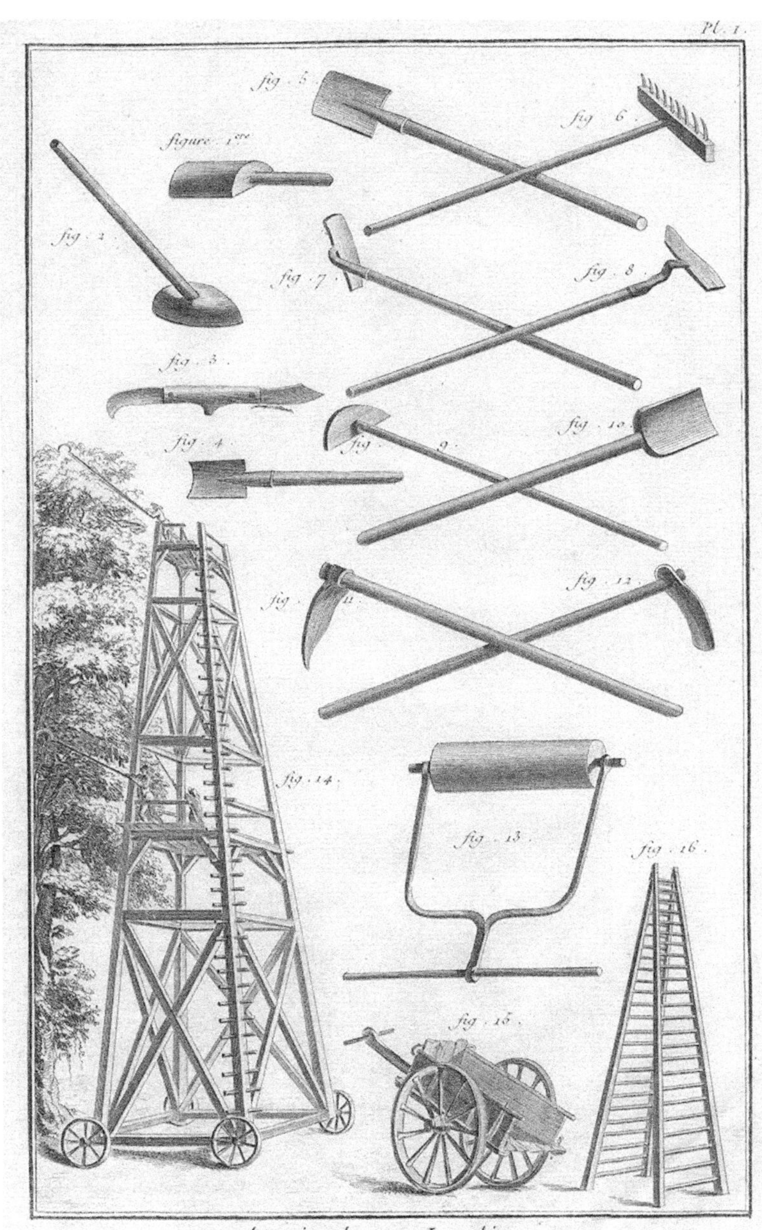
Pl. 1.
figure 1ere
fig. 2
fig. 3
fig. 4
fig. 5
fig. 6
fig. 7
fig. 8
fig. 9
fig. 10
fig. 11
fig. 12
fig. 13
fig. 14
fig. 15
fig. 16
Agriculture, Jardinage.

We have no
idea what
we're doing

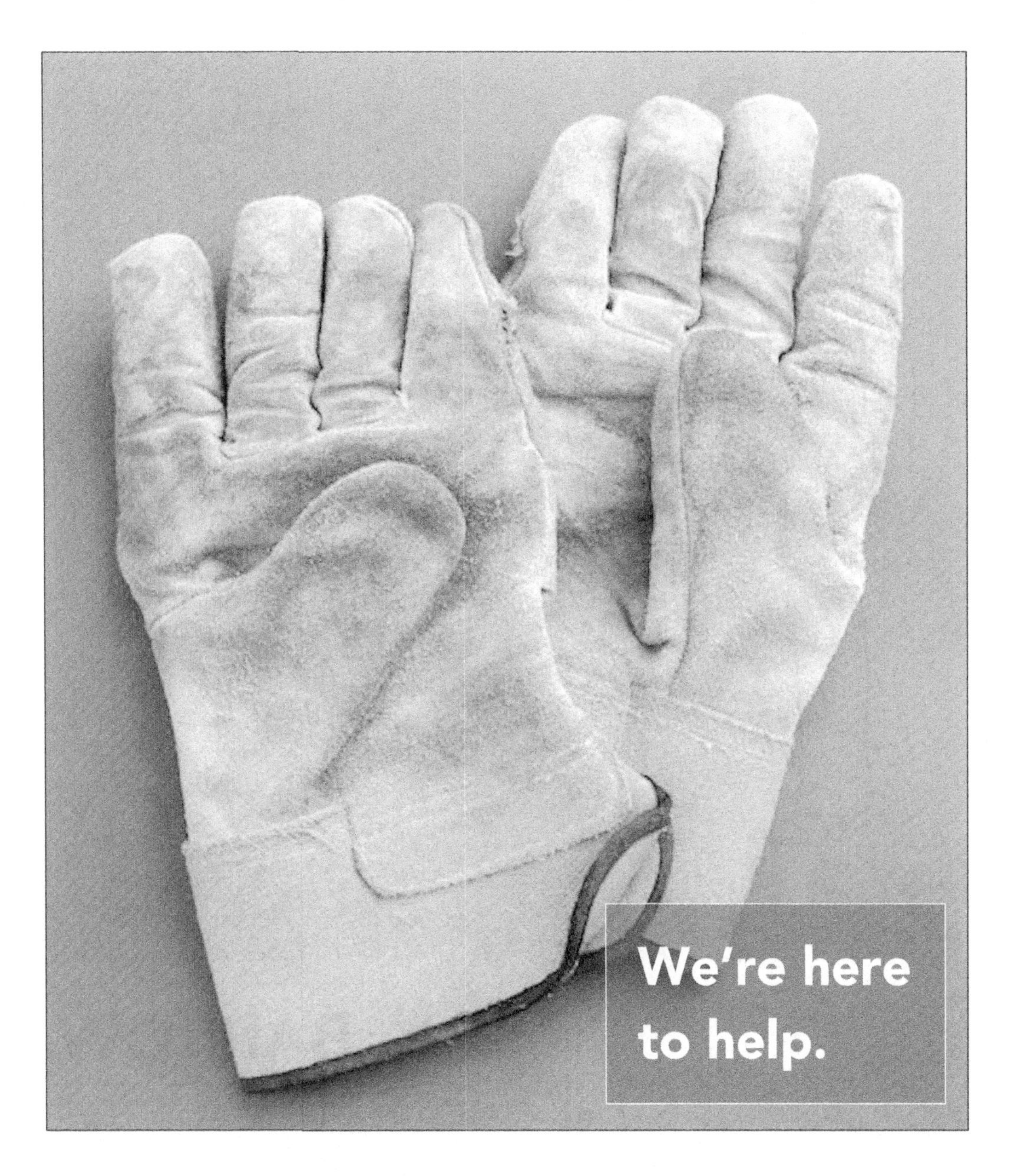
We're here
to help.

BARROW

WHEELBARROW

from Tim Allen

My Weirdest Tool

Q. What is the weirdest tool you ever bought?

A. Actually it was a garden shredder. A garden machine, but still a tool, right? It was a major deal. A freight company had to deliver it to my door. A big diesel Kenworth pulled up in front of my house and two burly guys hauled the shredder off the truck. The thing has a twelve-horsepower motor and is all tricked out. Here's what it does: It grinds up wood *right on your property*.

Okay, my wife did, too. I just wanted to get rid of all the twigs that had gathered during the year on my little acre-and-a-half. I've got a lot of big trees and they are always shedding. The guy made it look so easy on the commercial; his hair never moved. After using the shredder, the young couple on TV put the grounds in a blender and made mulch. They smiled all the while. You're supposed to put it on your junipers and related bushes. Unfortunately, I almost lost a leg trying to start the shredder because it was so powerful. And then it made so much noise just running I thought it was broken. So I got scared. All I could visualize was an index finger getting caught on one twig and then sucking me in like a guy who gets too close to the jet intake on an F-14. My wife told me she wasn't looking forward to tending my bloody stump just because I wanted to occasionally see the lawn. She also thought I was indulging in a little overkill.

"Aren't you using an atomic bomb to kill a mosquito?" Always so quick with a metaphor. "Just wrap up the twigs, take them to the street, and let the garbage man pick them up. I'm quite certain he won't break your leg or bloody your body. Better yet burn them. That means you get to play with fire!" She sure knows how to push my buttons.

It was good advice. Now the shredder is moldering in the shed, right next to the lawn tractor I don't use anymore.

— *Don't Stand Too Close to a Naked Man*

Winterizing your tools

We repeat: No sane person walks around in stiff new jeans, and the same thing goes for garden tools. Nothing says "I have zero idea what I'm doing" like a gleaming new set of tools, especially if you *are* just starting out.

So buy your tools used — very used. If your only option is buying them new, you'll want to "season" them first. Veteran gardeners recommend giving them a good dinging and scratching, then storing them outside year around.

German Peasants' War, 1524–1525

Big bags

It's been a tradition among veteran gardeners to migrate every spring to the local garden supply store or big box retailer to fill up trunks and back seats and flatbeds with bags of stuff — topsoil, potting mix, raised garden mix, mulch, and so on.

A few rare death-or-glory souls take their chances with sphagnum moss.

The bags lie stacked on wooden pallets in the parking lot. Big, 50-pound plastic bags — too unwieldy to put on a shopping cart, wheel inside, and take through the checkout line.

So the stores have abandoned that procedure.

"Just tell us now many bags you're taking," they

say. Then they calculate the charge, you pay them, and you drive away with all your big bags. Honors system.

Heck, the stores just leave the bags out in their parking lots overnight. No fence, no security.

Imagine stores doing this with other items. What could possibly go wrong?

But the only people who would want those big bags are gardeners.

And gardeners be honest folk.

DECIDING WHAT TO PLANT

Starting your garden? First determine the plants that will grow best in your garden. Choosing unsuitable plants will be like swimming upstream. You want to go with the flow.

Consider these questions:

- What is your growing region?
- What is the composition of your soil?
- What is your barometric pressure?
- What is your blood pressure?
- Is there shade in your garden during the day?
- Do you plan to itemize deductions or take the standard deduction?

For expert advice, call or visit your state extension representative to help you with these questions.

As for your growing region, she will feed key data points into her computer software, whose algorithms will tell you your zip code.

For your soil composition, if you send or take soil samples, she'll conduct CAT scans to determine your soil's "pH." She'll tell you if you have a cost basis to recover and need to report the transfer or rollover of your IRA or retirement plan on your tax return.

With the help of advanced computer software, she'll report — usually within 24 hours — what plants will thrive in your garden with the least effort on your part. Those plants are:

- rutabagas
- turnips
- Brussels sprouts
- eggplant
- rhubarb

As a rule, make a short list of the vegetables you abhor — these are the vegetables that will flourish in *your* garden.

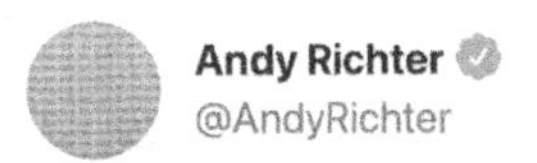

If you're going to buy plants from people who really know plants, be prepared to not fully understand why you are being scolded

Dear Miss Piggy,

For some reason,
my garden this year
produced a bumper
crop of cabbages,
and I don't know
what to do with them.
Are there any good
cabbage recipes?

Green Thumb

Dear Green Thumb,

No.

— Miss Piggy's Guide to Life

What you should plant

- Plant three rows of peas:
    - Peas of mind
    - Peas of heart
    - Peas of soul

- Plant four rows of squash:
    - Squash gossip
    - Squash indifference
    - Squash grumbling
    - Squash selfishness
- Plant four rows of lettuce:
    - Lettuce be faithful
    - Lettuce be kind
    - Lettuce be happy
    - Lettuce really love one another
- To conclude our garden: We must have thyme . . .
    - Thyme for fun
    - Thyme for rest
    - Thyme for ourselves

No garden should be without turnips . . .

- Turnip for service when needed
- Turnip to help one another
- Turnip the music and dance

Gardener's recipe

- One part soil
- Two parts water
- Three parts wishful thinking

— Unknown

When I see a plant reaching toward the sun, I'm just like, do you have any idea how desperate you look

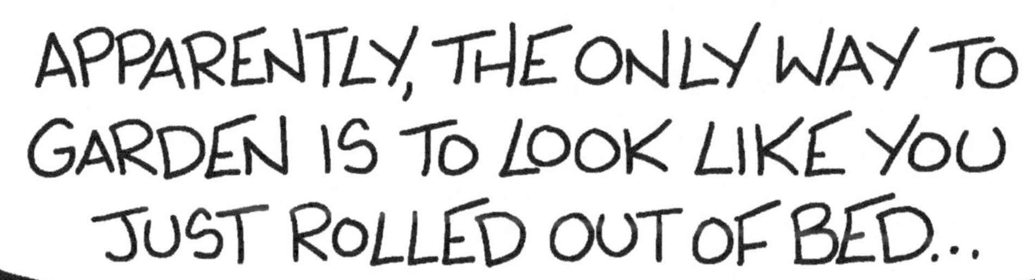

DENISE HAD SECOND THOUGHTS ABOUT THE SHADE PLANTS

from The Onion

NEWS IN BRIEF

Home Depot Introduces New 100-Pound Bag of Mulch for Fucking Up Back in Garden Section

ATLANTA—Touting the product as the easiest way for DIY-ers to seriously injure themselves, Home Depot introduced a new 100-pound bag of mulch Thursday for fucking up your back in the garden section. "Made from all-natural organic materials, our new too-heavy bag of mulch is perfect for absolutely destroying your spine the very first time you try to pick it up," said spokesperson Anthony Beasley, noting that the mulch bag's awkward dimensions and uneven weight distribution make it nearly impossible to carry by yourself. "Conveniently located on the cement floor so you can't get your hands underneath it, this bulk container of shredded wood will leave you doubled over in the garden section screaming, 'Son of a bitch!' Plus it's wet, so when it bursts open in the back of your SUV, it makes a huge ass mess. Weekend warriors who actually do manage to get it home will find this specific bag is somehow just barely not enough mulch to get the job done, requiring a return trip to Home Depot and another herniated disc." Home Depot also debuted a new line of delicate terra cotta planters that shatter upon being touched.

My friend suggested putting aged manure on my strawberries.
I did — and I've decided to switch back to whipped cream.

How vegans are made . . .

Grazing aphids

DiG THiS

Life's a garden — dig it.

— David Spade

The best way to garden is to put on a wide-brimmed straw hat and some old clothes, and with a hoe in one hand and a cold drink in the other, tell somebody else where to dig.

— Texas Bix Bender, *Don't Throw in the Trowel*

The best way to get a man to dig in a garden would be to call it a sand trap.

— Unknown

Son knows best

An older man living alone in the northern part of Ireland, whose only son was in prison, didn't have anyone to dig the soil in his garden so he could plant his potatoes. So he wrote to his son about his predicament.

The son sent this reply: "For heaven's sake, don't dig the garden up — that's where I buried the guns!"

At 3:00 am the next morning, a dozen British soldiers turned up and dug the garden for three hours — but didn't find any guns. They apologized to the man and left.

Confused, the man wrote to his son telling him what had happened, asking him what he should do now?

The son sent this reply: "NOW plant the potatoes!"

What goes
into your
compost . . .

And what
comes out.

DEFLOWERED

A gardener's fall fantasy of sex & death

by Meredith Siemsen

Each spring, about a week after I finish planting my flowerbeds and boxes, and everyone else's — my third job, essentially — I start counting the days until first frost. My enthusiasm for bountiful blooms wanes real quick when I remember it's up to me to keep everything alive for the next four months.

"Oh, whyyyy," I cry, "did I buy all of these stinkin' annuals!? What is wrong with me?" I sound like Elaine Benes as she breaks up with that idiot beefcake David Puddy for the seventh time on Seinfeld: 'THAT'S *IT!!* I cannot take this!!"

I make this solemn vow every summer: "I really am doing the bare-bones minimum next year, the absolute minimum." But, unfortunately, like a cat in heat who can't ignore her very nature, flower fever is a real thing for me in May — as is my inability to walk away from a perfectly good-looking four-pack that's just been given a death sentence on the sale rack at Walmart in June, or even mid-July. Some people collect shoes because they can't help themselves. Or boyfriends. Or cats. I collect flowers. They are my bébés.

But in the dog days, my potted pretties become neeeedy little babies. The ravenous rabbits, hellish heat, speckly spots, aphids and beetles, crappy drainage, and leaky hoses are just the tip of my woeful iceberg.

July brings funky, fried-up leaves, stressed-out roots, and paltry petals that are constantly whining for water or food or soap spray or neem oil, seeming to barely notice the care I so tenderly provide, like ungrateful teenagers. Even worse, those pestilent, post-pubescent plants begin a race against what's left of my personal time to create seeds, seeds, seeds — absolutely hell-bent on procreation. And once that happens, well, I've really lost the battle of beauty. A flower's lust for baby making takes the luster right out of it, and sure as anything, it's lost its bloom.

The hundreds — and I do mean hundreds — of petunias I'm in charge of each summer become controlling, colicky chlorophyll aliens in my own Little Shop of Horrors, probing my every thought from across town and demanding from me more and more of my blood, sweat, and occasionally even tears as the summer marches on.

Have you ever seen a petunia that's gone to seed? Not long after each blossom has withered brown and fallen to the ground, a petal-free pod poking out of a *Kermit* the Frog-like collar emerges, bearing a striking resemblance to Little Shop's Audrey *II,* the man-eating monster-weed from outer space. And every single one of its beak-like, seed-laden mouths is thirsty for murder as it cracks open and vomits up a little pile of black death. Don't be fooled by those remaining trumpets of color further down the stalk; that plant is trying to kill itself. Match the sadistic seed-making frenzy of a hundred prolific petunia plants with a sudden raging case of green aphids and you may as well hire yourself a NOLA brass band, because you've got yourself one hell of a funeral march on the way.

Petunia. Such a pretty word. So melodic. So innocent. Whatever.

She's the one committing suicide, but I'm the one with 63 chigger bites, premature sunspots, and forefinger callouses the size of Guam — from months of pinching off dead blossoms to stall the inevitable decline of someone I used to love. But, hey, at least I have the sexiest farmer's tan this side of the Skunk River.

This morning, August 4th, a shot of cold air came blasting through my bedroom window, an intoxicating cocktail of cool, reminding me that the end of summer is truly not far off. I got ready for my day, drunk with the happy thought of the sweaters I would soon be unpacking from storage, tucked away beside my favorite wool socks. Bring on the pies, the hot spiced teas, and the pumpkin everything. I dearly welcome the colorful gourds that will soon be replacing the chewed-up flowers on my porch. Those poor mangled blooms have been a constant, depressing reminder that the local herd of deer, the hungry zombies of the night,

have at last invaded my neighborhood and have turned it into an all-you-can-eat buffet
This month, or maybe next, I shall release my final caretaking tension with a satisfied cry, “Die, ye posies and fickle florets! I’ve given you the best of me. . . . I’m taking back the rest of me!”

I can stop carrying water. And I will stay in bed as long as I want.

Gardening is a kind of disease. It infects you, you cannot escape it. When you go visiting, your eyes rove about the garden; you interrupt the serious cocktail drinking because of an irresistible impulse to get up and pull a weed.

— Lewis Gannit

THE SUN: I am 100 million billion pounds of burning hydrogen, helium, carbon, neon, and iron.

PLANTS: Yum yum I’ll have that and a water.

PARSLEY, SAGE, ROSEMARY, & RHYME

This poem is attributed to Lady Maconochie of Inverewe. Inverewe is a botanical garden in the Scottish Highlands. She scorns visitors who make off with plants and cuttings, pronouncing curses on their gardens.

The Gardener's Curse

Awake, my muse, bring bell and book
To curse the hand that cuttings took.
May every sort of garden pest
His little plot of ground infest
Who stole the plants from Inverewe,
From Falkland Place, Grathes too.
Let caterpillars, capsid bugs,
Leafhoppers, thrips, all sorts of slugs,
Play havoc with his garden plot,
And a late frost destroy the lot.

Cabbage always has a heart

Cabbage always has a heart,
Green beans string along.
You're such a Tomato,
Will you Peas to me belong?
You've been the Apple of my eye,
You know how much I care.
So Lettuce get together,
We'd make a perfect Pear.
Now, something's sure to Turnip,
To prove you can't be Beet.
So, if you Carrot all for me
Let's let our Tulips meet.
Don't Squash my hopes and dreams now,
Bee my Honey, dear,
Or tears will fill Potato's eyes,
While Sweet Corn lends an ear.
I'll Cauliflower shop and say
Your dreams are Parsley mine.
I'll work and share my Celery,
So be my Valentine.

— Unknown

Roses are red

Violets are blue

Sunflowers are yellow

I bet you were expecting something romantic but no, this is just gardening facts

My special talent

When gardening, I have one gift
You won't find in any manuals —
I know it's strange, but I can change
Perennials to annuals.

— Dick Emmons

You might be a redneck if your baby's favorite teething ring is the garden hose in the front yard.
— Jeff Foxworthy

DASTARDLY WEEDS

Make no mistake, the weeds will win — nature bats last.

— Robert Michael Pyle

If dandelions were hard to grow, they would be most welcome on any lawn.

— Andrew V. Mason

You fight dandelions all weekend, and late Monday afternoon there they are, pert as all get out, in full and gorgeous bloom, pretty as can be, thriving as only dandelions can in the face of adversity.

— Hal Borland

It is not enough for a gardener to love flowers; he must also hate weeds.

— Anonymous

Nature abhors a garden.

— Michael Pollan

A weed is a plant that has mastered every survival skill except for learning how to grow in rows.

— Doug Larson

If you water it and it dies, it's a plant. If you pull it out and it grows back, it's a weed.

— Gerry Daly

A weed is a plant that is not only in the wrong place but intends to stay.

— Sara Stein

They know, they just know where to grow, how to dupe you, and how to camouflage themselves among the perfectly respectable plants, *they just know*, and therefore, I've concluded weeds *must* have brains.

— Dianne Benson, *Dirt*

Give a weed an inch and it will take a yard. — Unknown

The philosopher who said that work well done never needs doing over never weeded a garden.

— Ray D. Everson

HERE IS WHERE WE ESTABLISH A STRONGHOLD...
MARK PARISI

My basic weeding rule:
If they grow in rows they're flowers. If they don't they're weeds. — David Hobson

Why can't our garden plants be more like weeds?

- No cost
- Self-planting
- Self-propagating
- Perfectly at home in your microecosystem
- Disease and pest resistant
- No watering
- No pruning
- And no weeding!

Someone please remind us:
Why do we call these
glorious golden beauties
WEEDS?

Law of Gardening I:

When weeding, the best way to make sure you are removing a weed and not a valuable plant is to pull on it. If it comes out of the ground easily, it is a valuable plant.

Corollary:

To distinguish flowers from weeds, simply pull up everything. What grows back is weeds.

Would someone kindly reduce my soil pH just a bit?

A crack
in the
concrete!
OMG!

Take me to your
WEEDER

"I always arise from weeding a different person from the one who first knelt down." — Bronwyn Lea
Like when my back goes out.
BEHR
SATIN FLAT
HOUSE & TRIM

BOWERS OF FLOWERS

What's the truth about roses?

"They're blobs on sticks! They take far too much looking after to get a decent plant."

—Anne Wareham, famous English gardener and author

A man walks into a flower shop.

"I'd like some flowers, please."

"Certainly, sir. What did you have in mind?"

"Well, I'm not sure," he shrugs. "I uh, well . . . um, I. . . ."

"Perhaps I could help. What exactly have you done?"

from The Onion

NEWS IN BRIEF

Flower Freaking Out After Realizing There's A Bee On It

CAMILLA, GA — Remaining perfectly motionless despite its mounting terror, Zinnia peruviana FL77542PM4 found itself on the verge of panic Monday after noticing a honeybee had landed on one of its petals. "Oh, fuck. Oh, fuck me. Okay, deep breaths. Maybe it just wants to rest for a second and then it'll fly away," said the magenta-hued flower, trying to keep in mind that bees only sting when defending the hive, and to the best of its knowledge, it had not gone anywhere near one. "Shit, it must be attracted to my bright coloration. Oh, God, oh, God, it's going towards my stamen! I know it's irrational, but I'm sorry, I fucking hate these things." FL77542PM4 was later relieved when the bee flew away without incident, but freaked out again just moments later upon realizing it was standing right on top of a worm.

You know you are a hard-core gardener if you deadhead flowers in other people's gardens.

— Sue Careless

Anything for fun

Two older ladies were sitting on a park bench outside the local town hall where a flower show was in progress.

One leaned over and said, “Life is so boring. We never have any fun anymore. For $5.00 I’d take my clothes off right now and streak through that dumb flower show!”

“You’re on!” said the other, holding up a five-dollar bill.

The first lady pulled off her clothes and, completely naked, streaked through the front door of the flower show.

Waiting outside, her friend soon heard a huge commotion inside the hall, followed by loud applause. The naked lady burst out through the door surrounded by a cheering crowd.

“What happened?” asked her waiting friend.

“Why, I won first prize for Best Dried Arrangement.”

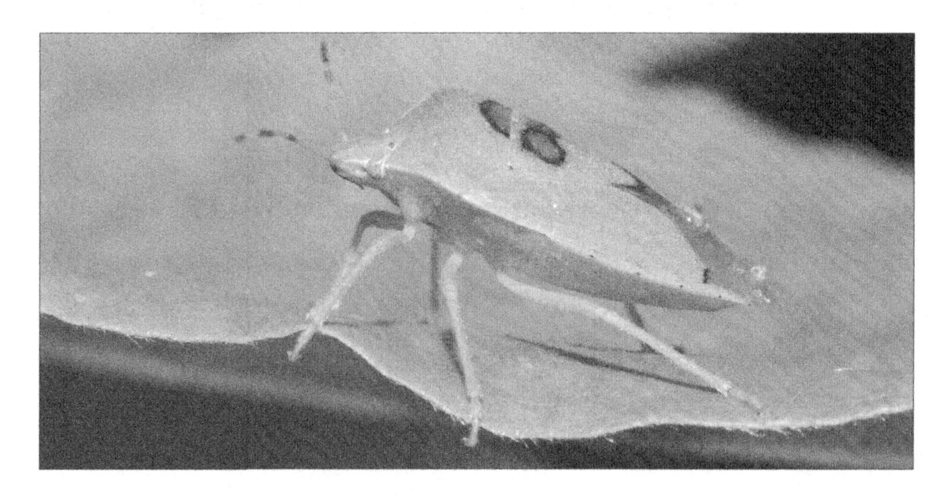

When you feel the world spinning out of control, take heart . . .

There's an orchid called **Hanging Naked Men** (orchis italica).

"A rose is a rose is a rose."
— Gertrude Stein

"A hose is a hose is a hose."
— Gertrude Stern

Dozing bumblebees with pollen on their bottoms

HI, MOLLY!
JULIE?
SHERYL?
MITZI?
MARK PARISI
MARCELLA WAS DISAPPOINTED IN HER FORGET-ME-NOTS
©2020 Mark Parisi Dist by Andrews McMeel
offthemark.com

HOW DO YOU MEASURE UP?

Here are some statistics from the National Gardening Association about the average American gardener. But don't compare your situation with these figures — experts say comparing yourself with others only brings misery and pain.

The average American gardener . . .

- is female
- is over 45 years old
- has a college degree or some college education (79% chance)
- has a 600-square-foot garden
- spends an average of 5 hours per week working in it
- spends about $70 on gardening each year
- grows $600 worth of food

The most grown veggies

- 86% – tomatoes
- 47% — cucumbers
- 46% — sweet peppers
- 39% — beans
- 34% — carrots
- 32% — summer squash
- 32% — onions
- 31% — hot peppers
- 28% — lettuce
- 24% — peas
- 23% — sweet corn
- N/A — rutabagas
- N/A — turnips
- N/A — brussels sprouts
- N/A – eggplant
- N/A – okra

WHY GARDENING IS BETTER THAN SEX

- Gardeners are not embarrassed explaining the birds and the bees to their kids.
- If your regular gardening partner isn't available, he or she won't object if you garden with someone else.
- It's acceptable to garden before you're married.
- The Ten Commandments say nothing against gardening.
- You don't have to shower and shave before gardening.
- No matter how old you are, you'll always be able to garden.
- You'll never hear anyone say: "Is gardening all you ever think about?"
- You don't have to hide your *Gardening* magazines.
- Telling gardening jokes and inviting coworkers to garden with you is not considered workplace harassment.

- Email with gardening content is not considered offensive.
- When you become famous, you don't have to worry about photos and videos of you gardening showing up on the Internet.
- Your gardening partner doesn't get upset about people you gardened with a long time ago.
- It's perfectly respectable to enjoy gardening with a total stranger.
- When you see a good gardener, you don't have to feel guilty about imagining the two of you gardening together.
- Every time you garden, you hope to produce fruit.
- Nobody will ever tell you you'll go blind if you garden by yourself.
- When dealing with a gardening pro, you never have to wonder if they're really an undercover cop.
- You don't have to go to a sleazy shop in a seedy neighborhood to buy gardening stuff.
- You can have a gardening related calendar on your wall at the office.
- There are no gardening-transmitted diseases.
- No one objects if you watch the gardening channel on television.
- Nobody expects you to garden with the same person your whole life.

- Nobody expects you to give up gardening if your partner loses interest.
- You don't have to be a newlywed to plan a vacation primarily to enjoy your favorite activity.
- Your partner will never say, "Not again? We just gardened last week!"

It's Mother Nature's way of telling me flowers get more sex than I do.

— Basil White on why he dislikes allergy season

PLANTEN
Why do men go to bars to meet women?
At garden centers there are ten women for every man.
And those women are already looking for things they don't need.

Only in England

Actual names of ancient varieties of fruit grown in England, but struggling to survive:

- **Hens' Turds apple** — said to produce an excellent cider, also good for cooking and jelly
- **Bloody Bastard pear** — a red-fleshed pear verging on extinction
- **Shit Smock plum** — a small green fruit — "The name indicates the fate of the garments of young fellows who over-indulged."
- **Gilliflower of Gloucester** — a dessert apple
- **Arlingham Schoolboys** — an apple named after a village in Gloucester

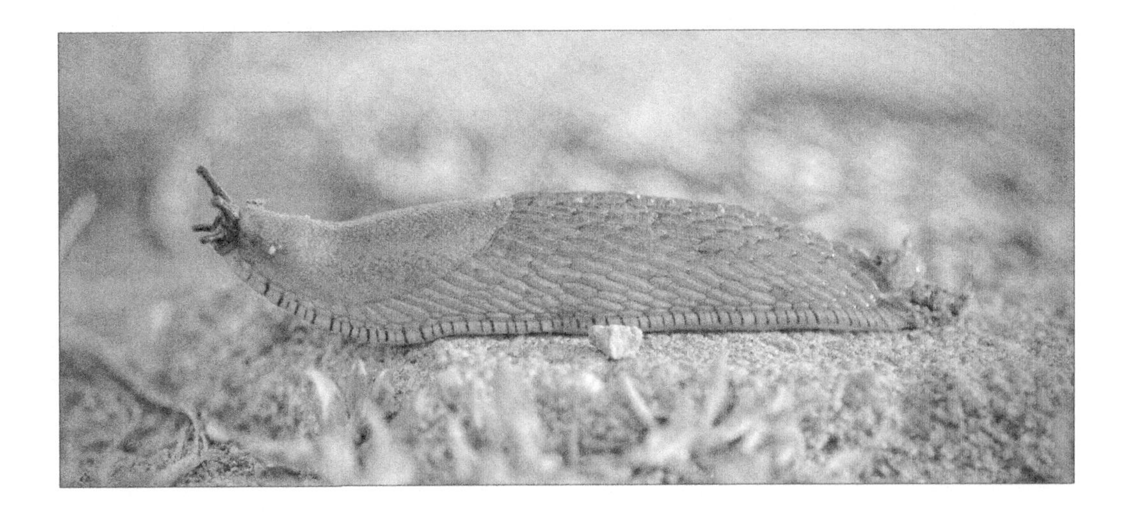

OH, DON'T MIND LARRY
HE'S A LITTLE INVASIVE...
MARK PARISI
©2019 Mark Parisi Dist by Andrews McMeel Synd.
offthemark.com

TiP TALK

Enter the gardening world, and you enter a world of *tips* — bits of information every gardener is supposed to know. How to do this . . . when to do that . . . where to do this . . . why you do that.

In the gardening world, tips are everywhere — in seed and gardening catalogs, in gardening magazines, on gardening websites and blogs and other gardening social media, on seed packets, carved into shovel handles and etched into shovel blades.

Go into any gardening store and you'll hear tips, tips, and more tips — in the conversations among employees and customers, in the aisles among the customers themselves, over the PA system.

Go to parties with gardeners and all the chit chat will be gardening tips.

Tips, tips, tips.

The exchange of gardening tips can work its way into any situation.

SCENE:

A city park, Sunday morning. Two friends are walking their dogs and happen to cross paths.

BERNIE: Hey, Herb! Haven't seen you in a while. How's it going?

HERB: I'm fine, Bernie. You know, the best time to divide and transplant spring-blooming perennials is in the late summer or early autumn. And how have *you* been?

BERNIE: Doing great, Herb. By the way, if your rhubarb plants are sending up flower stalks, you want to be sure to remove them — you want your rhubarb to focus on producing foliage, not seeds.

HERB: And be sure you know your USDA "hardiness zone" so you don't plant things that won't make it through the winter.

BERNIE: Good to see you, Herb. You take care.

HERB: See ya, Bernie.

SCENE:

Front hallway of a home. The mother is sending her seven-year-old daughter off to school.

MOM: All right, Lucy, off you go now. Look both ways before you cross the street, and don't forget that it usually takes perennials three years after you plant them to reach their mature size. I love you.

LUCY: Love you too, Mom. The best way to keep weeds out of the garden is weeding and hand-hoeing.

MOM: That's my girl!

LUCY: And sphagnum moss is a good medium for growing succulents indoors.

MOM: (pausing and frowning slightly)
Lucy, how do you know about sphagnum? We have never had any, and Dad and I have never, ever spoken of it.

LUCY: (smiles and shrugs)

MOM: (another pause and frown, then brightening)
Okay, off to school! Love you!

SCENE:

US Highway 44 between Oklahoma City and Tulsa. Bob is driving east, listening to a podcast, when he sees rapidly flashing blue and red lights zooming up behind him. He looks at his speedometer. Yikes! — he's been going 90 miles an hour for the last couple of minutes. Heart pounding, he pulls onto the shoulder, with the highway patrol car pulling off just ahead. The officer gets out and walks back to Bob's window.

OFFICER: Where you headed, sir?

BOB: To Chicago actually, to visit my mother.

OFFICER: You were going a little fast.

BOB: I'm so sorry. I had cruise control set to 75, the speed limit, and I was listening to a podcast and got so excited I must have accidentally put my foot on the accelerator.

OFFICER: What podcast?

BOB: The Joe Gardener Show.

OFFICER: Joe Lamp'l? "Organic Gardening Like a Pro"?

BOB: That's the one. You know about him?

OFFICER: Which episode?

BOB: This one's called "Hydrangea Care for Late Winter: Pro Tips for Pruning and More, With Lorraine Ballato."

OFFICER: (smiling broadly)
Ah. Well. You want to prune your Big Leaf Hydrangea during the summer, after the flowers have started fading but before

August. Same with Oakleaf if you want to control its size or shape. But your Smooth and Peegee and Limelights, you want to prune those guys in the spring, before the buds appear.

BOB: That's really expert advice, officer — thank you.

OFFICER: OK, you take care now and have a good trip home. Pick up some hydrangeas for your mama, you hear?

SCENE:

College basketball locker room, halftime during the playoffs. The players are gathered with the coach.

COACH: Guys, State was supposed to blow us out of the water in this game — and we're up by three points! *We're playing right with them — and we've got the momentum. You can do this!* But remember: If you're applying manure to your soil, be sure it cures for at least six months and is fully composted and rotted — otherwise the high nitrogen content can actually 'burn' your plants."

PLAYER: Fresh manure can also harbor parasites and pathogens.

COACH: Great tip, Eddie. That's the leadership that inspired your teammates to elect you team captain.

PLAYER: What about pig, dog, and cat manure?

COACH: Never put any of that in your compost pile or garden — it could hold parasites that can infect humans. Now go out there and *win this thing!*

SCENE:

Harry and Sally's bedroom, Saturday night. Harry and Sally are young professionals, thirty-somethings, smart, beautiful, athletic. They've just spent the day working in their garden and have climbed into bed together.

SALLY: What a beautiful day we had.

HARRY: We sure did. Loved it. Love you.

SALLY: Harry?

HARRY: Yeah?

SALLY: Harry, would you do that thing I like?

HARRY: Do you mean —

SALLY: Yes. Do it now — *please.*

HARRY: (leaning closer and whispers in her ear)
Aphids can be controlled with a strong shot of water from the hose or by spraying the leaves with insecticidal soap.

SALLY: Oh, I love it when you talk like that.

HARRY: Be sure to prune fruit and flower-bearing trees every spring, or else they won't produce a yield — but also wait to prune until *after* the last frost.

SALLY: Oh God. . . .

HARRY: Neem oil does wonders for preventing pests and fungus on fruit trees in the spring.

SALLY: *Oh my God. . . .*

HARRY: If you save the leaves you rake in the fall and add them to your compost, you can make the compost so much richer.

SALLY: Oh my God, oh my God, oh my God. . . Harry . . . This is amazing . . . Are you feeling it too?

HARRY: I'm right with you, Sally.

SALLY: Do it harder, Harry.

HARRY: Banana peels improve compost piles by adding valuable phosphorus, which helps plants fend off heat, cold, disease, and other stressors.

SALLY: Oh . . . oh my God. Harder, Harry, harder.

HARRY: **And coffee grounds will provide your pile with the valuable nutrients magnesium and potassium, which support new plant growth, improve plants' ability to ward off disease and resist drought.**

SALLY: (Energy rises up her spine)
A little softer now, Harry.

HARRY: *A raised garden will enable you to start your garden earlier and garden longer.*

SALLY: (The current of energy reaches her forehead and explodes into a billowing cloud of golden, iridescent light, filling every cell of Sally's body with divine, vibrating love and bliss)
Harry . . . Harry. . . .

HARRY: Planting winter wheat will help prevent weeds through the winter and spring, and in the spring you can spade it into your soil and add vital nutrients.

SALLY: (The cloud has expanded in every direction to infinity, Sally floating in the center, realizing her cosmic oneness with the universe, infinite, eternal, immortal)

HARRY: To attract bees, plant catmint, calendula, and bee palm. . . .

SALLY: Ahh. . . .

Growing Chefs!
@growingchefsBC
Gardening just got a little more rock'n'roll #puns #garden
Watch Robert Plant
while Roger Waters.

"I planted some birdseed. A bird came up. Now I don't know what to feed it.
— Steven Wright

THE GARDENING MADNESS TEST

by Susan M. Watkins

Take this test to see if you are truly a Mad Gardener or merely an ordinary human being.

1. Your ideal garden is:

(a) The carefully tended rose garden at Bennington-Barrington von Hereford-Hampshire Estates, Shropespume, England.

(b) A neat planting of wax begonias surrounded by sterilized white gravel-encircling the base of the central air-conditioning unit.

(c) A single-file strip of marigolds and petunias mixed with red-hot poker plants bordering your sidewalk along with Porky Pig and Minnie Mouse holding plastic whirling sunflowers with Day-Glo yellow petals and a hilarious wooden bent-over buttboard suggesting that the resident female is both meaty and immodest.

d) All over the place in every available nook and cranny of your yard, sometimes with vegetables and flowers in the same plot, or in pots all over your porch, or anywhere else you can possibly put some dirt.

(e) Somewhere else.

2. Your favorite gardening activity is:

(a) Assigning the weeks pruning and lawning duties to your impeccably attired Gardening Staff.

(b) Getting the driveway hosed off before cocktail hour arrives.

(c) Picking the discarded cigarette butts off the backs of your Velcro Yard Sheep.

(d) Sidedressing the bok choy with wheelbarrow loads full of homemade compost and observing the healthy millipede population within.

(e) Huh?

3. You budget your gardening expenses by:

(a) Allowing your accountant to depreciate the value of your Tasmanian soil technician's social security payments, thus gaining annuities on the plus side of your fiscal deductions.

(b) Purchasing the same two kinds of flowers year after year, so you know exactly what to expect.

(c) Buying your geraniums at garage sales and keeping the Dixie Cup container pots for refrigerator leftover dishes.

(d) Adding your monthly income to the "unused credit" portion of your Mastercard account and subtracting the total cost of purchases from all order forms that you filled out last year and hope to fill out this year, vowing that whatever is left over will be specifically earmarked for rent, food, taxes, and insurance.

(e) What?

4. You attend your town's annual Fourth of July parade. To you, the piles left behind in the street by the horses are:

(a) A damned fine argument for animal diapers.

(b) A substance completely foreign to your everyday existence.

(c) A good time for the street crew to start earning its overburdened-taxpayer-sonofa-funded-goddamned-bitching-minimum-wage hourly pay scale.

(d) The reason you brought along a shovel and bushel basket, and you hope nobody else has the same idea, because it looks to be exactly the right consistency to mix in with the load of chicken feathers and sawdust you had delivered last week from the organic egg factory.

(e) Poop.

5. You go out to a nice restaurant for a pleasant dinner with friends. Suddenly, you notice that you forgot to clean your filthy fingernails. You:

(a) Hastily exit to the loo, where you spend at least fifteen minutes scrubbing with the nail brush that you always carry on your person just in case of accidental digital contamination.

b) Are on your third martini along with everybody else, so nobody notices and you have forgotten what the question was.

(c) Put your hands in your lap and dig at the dirt with your fork and dinner napkin, which you then use to blow your nose and wipe off your forehead.

(d) Draw attention to the condition of your nails by explaining that you prefer to turn your compost heap by hand every three weeks without fail and that this afternoon's turn was especially fruit with baby red wiggler maggots.

(e) Have got to be kidding

Which garden do you identify with? This? . . .

6. Worms are:

(a) Mildly disgusting though probably necessary invertebrates that exist somewhere near the bottom of the Evolutionary Ladder of Social Progress and Civilized Deportment.

(b) The things responsible for creating those swirly patterns that highlight the veneer of your triumphantly expensive faux antique coffee table.

(c) Bait, or more to the point, your Ex. Hopefully both.

(d) Saviors of the soil and among your favorite creatures. You are careful not to hurt them with shovels and you always pick them off hot sidewalks and return them to the nearest dirt patch.

(e) Catching.

7. Woodchucks are:

(a) Mammals of the order Rodentia, characterized by an insufferable propensity to undermine the flooring beneath the winetasting gazebo, thus scaring the wits out of poor Muffy.

(b) Those little scorekeeping pins you use on cribbage boards probably.

(c) Your uncle Gomer's favorite moving targets, not to mention dinner and hat material.

Or this? . . .

(d) Harmlessly repelled using the latest mail-order catalog electrical fencing devices now on sale for only $379.95 plus $32 shipping and handling.

(e) Oh, I don't know, sort of cute. Aren't they?

8. Catalogs are:

(a) Delivered to you periodically from Sotheby's to keep you apprised of items upon which you might wish to offer sealed bids, if they are not imposing upon your time too awfully much.

(b) Easier than driving all the way up to Mr. Bean's nice little store in that quaint little town in, where is it? New Hampshire?

(c) Stuck in the Sunday newspaper with all those coupons that Grandma likes to cut out and save.

(d) Probably the most wonderful invention of the twentieth century, aside from, maybe, birth control and the microwave oven.

(e) A real pain in the neck. You can get fined for throwing them out in the trash, for the luvva gawd.

9. A true test of your boyfriend's commitment to your relationship is:

(a) Showing up when promised to unplug your toilet and/or septic tank.

(b) Willingness to run to the store and buy tampons for you in emergency situations.

(c) Not commenting out loud about inevitable male-mind connection between (a) and (b).

(d) Not jumping up to put on pants and run downstairs to for crying out loud something five seconds after finished with another of those typically insensitive male-oriented afternoon quicWE INTERRUPT THIS RESPONSE TO BRING YOU A SPECIAL BULLETIN. THIS QUESTION RECENTLY ESCAPED FROM NEW WOMAN MAGAZINE AND WAS APPREHENDED WHILE SEEKING REFUGE IN THE PAGES OF THIS BOOK. WE APOLOGIZE FOR ANY INCONVENIENCE THIS MAY HAVE CAUSED. THANK YOU AND HAVE A NICE DAY.

10. In winter, you pass the time waiting for gardening season by:

(a) Enjoying the view off the terrace overlooking the Queen's' Royal Arboretum of Cairo.

(b) Playing bridge with the Dysons and sewing skirts for the dried flower baskets you're making for the country club's spring charity luncheon.

c) Driving the camper-trailer to Disney World so you can stand in line for six hundred hours for the privilege of floating through the Future Moon City FlowerScape display on a plastic boat piloted by Goofy.

(d) Reading, and ordering out of, more catalogs than there are trees on the entire planet and for that matter ever were on the entire planet and certainly ever will be again.

(e) Z-Z-Z-Z-Z-Z-Z-Zzzzzzzzzzzflbbbsflbbbabbllllllzzzzz

11. Your garage does not contain any garden tools. This is because:

(a) You do not have a "garage." You have a "carriage house."

(b) Your Neighborhood Beautification Committee voted against allowing anything in garages except hose-holders and clean, late model cars.

(c) There is no room in the garage, what with the RV and the gas grill and the busted washing machine and the leftovers from Ma's rummage sale last year.

(d) They are all kept out in the gardening shed, next to the garden.

(e) Garden *what*?

12. Besides grass, your front yard contains:

(a) The electronically controlled wrought iron gate and guardhouse.

(b) Nothing.

(c) A collection of colorful plastic flamingos and gnomes, one of which holds a sign declaring that your family, along with a grammatically incorrect apostrophe, lives here.

(d) An ecologically friendly mailbox and sixteen flowering trees.

(e) You don't know.

13. Your compost pile is:

(a) Located somewhere out behind the riding stables. You'll have to ask Mr. Yoto when he comes in from the rose hedge.

(b) Not allowed in your neighborhood, thank God.

(c) Kind of all over the yard. Maybe some on the porch and down between the stove and the sink. Does the spot under the TV tray-table count?

(d) Your life's pride and joy. You cheer it on when it heats up in the spring. You turn it over just for the thrill of sniffing its earthy odors. You write notes about its progress on Christmas cards. You carry pictures of it in your wallet.

(d) My what???

14. Your grass clippings are:

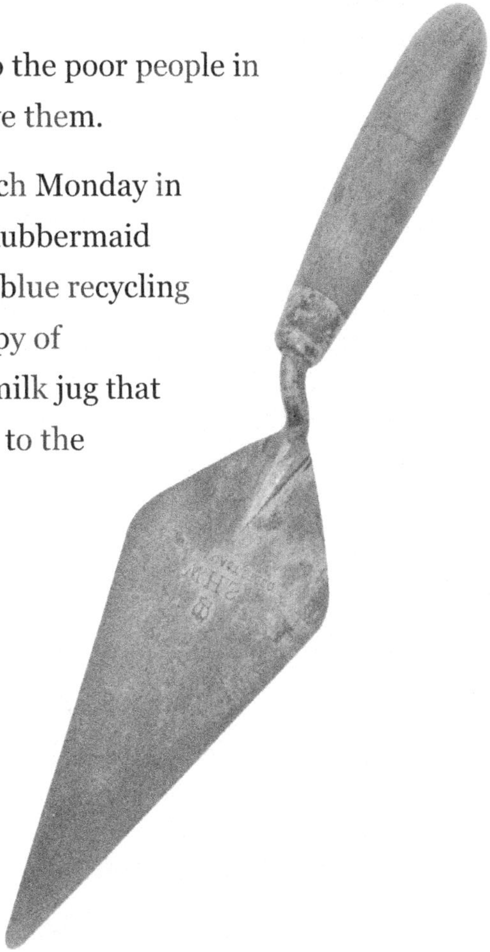

(a) Taken up in bundles and shipped to the poor people in India, who are jolly well grateful to have them.

(b) Carefully placed on the curbside each Monday in clear plastic bags alongside the three Rubbermaid snap-top trash cans on wheels and the blue recycling box, which this week contained one copy of National Geographic and a #2 plastic milk jug that you rinsed out and flattened according to the rules.

(c) Since you haven't gotten around to mowing the lawn in five or six weeks, you don't have any grass clippings. In fact, you can't even find the lawnmower. Last time you looked, it was out behind the doghouse.

(d) Left on the lawn or layered in the compost pile, where they belong.

(e) Oh, criminy, what now, another citation?

15. A severe storm sends damaging wind, rain, and hailstones across the land. Afterward, you:

(a) Instruct Jeeves to send condolences to old Grimes, the Yard Man who sees to the raking. What with the poor codger's arthritis and all, it certainly was a spot of bloody rotten luck, wasn't it?

(b) Speak to your insurance representative when you meet at the club for your Thursday morning foursome at nine.

(c) Spend a couple of days propping the Holy Mother's blue-painted bathtub back up where it belongs in the coleus shrine.

(d) Realize that the forces of Nature are part of the cycle of life, and that broken-off blossoms and branches will make fine additions to the compost heap, at least.

(e) Complain to the cable company about power outages during *Wide World of Sports.*

16. Hordes of insect pests are attacking your vegetables and flowers. You:

(a) Have already left for the Opening Day Races at Ascot Downs, so you are not available to answer this question.

(b) Happen 10 run into the town supervisor's wife at the church bazaar, where you have a chat about upcoming aerial spraying schedules, during which you will of course stay indoors and make canapes.

(c) Douse your whole yard with that stuff that What's-His-Name, you know, that grizzly old actor on TV, said you could hook up to your watering hose and blast the bejeezus out of the little bastard bugs and you wind up with seventy-five-pound radishes at the County Fair.

(d) Do nothing, other than hand-pick a few of the more obvious offenders off your tomato leaves, leaving your well-mulched and carefully weeded darlings to defend themselves with their own glowing organic fitness and health.

(e) Could not possibly care less, except maybe if you were dead.

17. To dress for gardening, you put on your:

(a) Best face, to properly encourage the help.

(b) Green and pink-striped culottes and green polo shirt with the alligator pocket and topsiders with bunny-tail socks. This is the way you dress for everything, including gardening, golfing, and sex.

(c) Old jeans that occasionally cover up almost all of the crack in your butt.

(d) Nikkis khaki garden pants, W. Atlee Burpees cotton garden tee shirt, Smith & Hawken's plastic garden clogs, Garden Supply's padded garden knee pads, Gardens Alive's gripper-ripper fitted garden gloves, Whiteflower Farms imported Colombian liana-brimmed garden hat, J.I. Rodale Book Club's organic gardening sunscreen, and Your Friendly Credit Card Collection Protection Services fake nose and mustache gardening disguise.

(e) To dress for what?

18. Your utility vehicle looks like:

(a) A mirror.

(b) Everyone else's Chrysler minivan.

(c) A four-by-four Dodge Rammit Badboy with eighty-eight DualDexter mag wheels, a six-sixty Souper Charger under the hood, and a rack for the ole double-barrel. No piece a'crap Japan pickup in *this* driveway you better believe.

(d) A piece of crap Toyota pickup with a bungee cord holding up the tailgate.

(e) A beer cooler.

19. You inherited your gardening consciousness from:

(a) Sir Aston Piticott Courteney Abernathy IV, the Earl of Gloucestershire, Knight of the Royal Argyle, and 19th in line for ascension to the Throne.

(b) Permitted Landscaping Model Number Three.

(c) The old lady's great-grandpa Derndorf, who left her the blue looker ball when he croaked.

(d) Your mother, who took you on walks through the woods when you were a child so you could look at the wildflowers and listen to the birds and later talk about what you saw while you helped her weed the beautiful annual and perennials beds that she created by sprouting inexpensive seeds on bricks placed in pans of water on the windowsills, a feat that in its simplicity seems almost mystical to you now.

(e) Television.

20. You would describe your gardening life as:

(a) Noblessedly obligeable.

(b) Pleasantly predictable.

(c) More fun than a fart in a mitten.

(d) More than the Ethereal sum of its Heavenly parts.

(e)

Scoring

For every "a" you selected, give yourself five points; for every "b" ten points; for every "c," fifteen points; for every "d," twenty points; and for every "e," twenty-five points.

Add up your score and rate yourself as follows:

5–100: BRITISH DEVOLVED — You fancy enormous hedges trimmed, by others, to resemble mythological beasts, and typically reside in domiciles larger than the entire downtown section of Albany, N.Y. Your garden is characterized by ramrod-straight hedgerows and geometrically precise pathways paralleled by rose bushes that are trimmed daily with tweezers, nose hair scissors, and whisk brooms. You employ squadrons of garden help and thus often wear wool clothing in the middle of July without discomfort. In fact, you do everything without discomfort, such as inspecting the arborvitae from the tinted window of your chauffeured limousine. In your leisure time you are the editor of a prestigious gardening magazine that would vomit, collectively speaking, if it saw what was crawling around inside the food-scraps pail currently residing in my kitchen sink.

You do not even know that the people in these other categories exist.

100–200: AMERICAN SUBURBAN — Gardening is not so much a pastime for you as it is an exterior decorating skill. You enjoy neatness and uniformity in all things, including your flowers, which are carefully lined up around flagpoles and patio edges and never vary in color or kind from year to year. Your backyard vegetables consist of two neatly staked hybrid tomato plants, whose yield you dutifully put by every fall in the form of relishes, chutneys, and jellies, which you give as Christmas presents in Williams-Sonoma catalog jars with preprinted "Specially Grown By" labels embossed on the tops. While one might see an occasional white iron bench reposing alongside your azaleas, you would never stick inspiring statuettes or wooden anatomical effigies in your yard, mainly because your Neighborhood Landscaping Committee would have your real anatomicals on a platter if you even joked about doing such a thing.

You adore, and are in fact required to have, a bright green, uniformly weedless, totally chemicalized front lawn.

200–300: AMERICAN GOTHIC – You enjoy colorful landscaping featuring old toilets and blue tractor tires with petunias growing out of them, and other interesting lawn decorations made from recycled materials such as bus seats and/or plumbing. Your vegetable garden consists of tomatoes stuck in black plastic kettles, runner beans crawling up the rainspouts, and blistering hot little peppers hilariously destined to incinerate everyone's digestive tract at the annual firehouse Chili Wars this summer. You own enormous over-financed pickup trucks that have flame decals and chrome hood-locks affixed upon them to express your patriotic attitude, although you rarely use these vehicles to transport anything but deceased wildlife and the weapons needed to dispatch them. You are the mainstay and the backbone of America, particularly that portion of this Great Land that makes a living from stick-in-the-ground cartoon characters whose legs spin around with every passing breeze.

You are very likely the happiest people alive on the planet today.

300–400: THE GARDENING MAD — Ah, yes. You are the ones who send away for worms and stinging insects advertised in mail-order catalogs. You are the ones who devote yourselves to the love and lore of composting and its materials; of hoeing and deadheading and digging and planting, and of thinking deeply about it and planning to do and buy and gather even more of everything, winter and summer, including, or especially, large quantities of steaming pig manure, which you consider an extremely fascinating topic of conversation. You may also believe in such things as gardening by the moon, holistic blackberry enemas for curing headaches, and the possibility of a balanced federal budget in your personal lifetime. You are, let us say, idealistic. . . . Anyway, you are smitten, and that's all there is to it.

You may request to be buried with trowel and claw crossed over your bosom and an onion on each of your eyes.

400+ NEVERMIND — I don't know who you people are at all. I don't even know what you are doing here. . . . In the meanwhile, those of you who scored in this category can go back to whatever it was that you were doing before this test came along. I'm sure it was every bit as worthwhile as gardening, such as figuring out how to buy the airspace over Wal-Mart, or planning the industrial development of Tierra del Fuego, or whatever.

— *Garden Madness: The Unpruned Truth About a Blooming Passion*

PROCEED TO THE ROOT...
©2018 Mark Parisi Dist by Andrews McMeel Synd.
offthemark.com

The longer I garden,
the more I love
manure.

HUMUS TO HUMOROUS

The truth comes out?

One morning a customer entered my flower shop and ordered a bouquet for his wife.

"No card is needed," he told us. "She'll know who sent them."

The delivery truck hadn't even returned to the store when the phone rang. It was the customer's wife.

"Who sent the flowers?" she asked.

After explaining that the customer had requested that no card be included, I considered the matter closed — but not so. A bit later, she came rushing in the front door.

"You've got to tell me who sent the flowers," she demanded, "before my husband gets home for lunch!"

Getting antsy?

For a number of years I worked with my Aunt Grace in the local library.

Part of my responsibility was to care for the plants, but Aunt Grace was forever overwatering them or trimming them unnecessarily.

One evening I was telling my husband about Aunt Grace's disastrous attentions when our daughter walked in.

"What's annoying mom?" she asked.

"I think you could say," my husband replied, "that she has aunts in her plants."

Sod off

At the garden center a customer ordered several rolls of sod. After ringing up the purchase I told him the total.

"That's too expensive," he said.

"But it includes tax," I replied, trying to be helpful.

"I don't think I'll need tacks," he said slowly. "It should stay down by itself."

Blast from the past

We had so many cucumbers we were having trouble finding different ways to use them up. Neither my mother nor I wanted to make one huge batch of something we'd be eating forever, so I was digging through all

Mom's recipe books for new and interesting ideas.

After hours of work, we had whittled the piles down to a manageable level. Finally, I found yet another relatively simple recipe and showed it to Mom.

She started laughing.

She had contributed it to a community book published for fund-raising and had later bought a copy to help out. She had forgotten the recipe and hadn't looked at the booklet in 30 years.

Sold!

Driving along a residential street, I spotted a little girl on the edge of the sidewalk clutching an armful of daisies and dandelions, which she was obviously trying to sell.

I stopped and asked how much she charged for her flowers.

Holding out a bunch, she answered, "If it's just for somebody you're giving them to, it's five cents, but if it's for somebody you like it's ten cents, but if it's for somebody you. . . ."

At that point, I produced a quarter and said, "I'm sold. What can I buy for this?"

Without hesitation, she handed me the whole bunch and accepted the quarter.

But before heading for the candy store, she looked up, smiled and said, "It's nice to sell my flowers to someone who is going to give them to somebody he loves."

Music to our ears

The selling and selecting of watermelons in the South becomes a way of life in summer. Just about every one of my customers thumps many melons before making a final selection, but no one can ever agree on exactly what the proper sound of a ripe melon should be.

One afternoon a blind man, a piano tuner by trade, came into my store to choose his melon. He felt and thumped some of the larger melons, but he always returned to the same one.

Then, with two final resounding thumps, he announced, "B flat! I'll take it!"

Mixed messages

A local florist just went out of business, but it was his own fault. He kept getting his orders mixed up.

One woman received flowers sent by her husband, who was at a business meeting in Florida. She was perplexed by the message on her card: "Our deepest sympathy."

But she was not nearly as surprised as the woman whose husband had just passed away. Her card read, "Hotter here than I expected. Too bad you didn't come too."

The customer is always right

I was selling surplus vegetables from our garden at the farmers' market.

Toward the end of the season, some of the otherwise delicious sweet corn began to show a little caterpillar damage at the tips. If I noticed such imperfections, I'd put a bonus ear into each customer's bag.

One busy Saturday I gave an extra ear to each of two customers in succession, then noticed that the third in line was a particularly picky buyer. Hoping to avoid criticism, I carefully selected twelve perfect ears for her.

It was the wrong strategy.

"How come you gave me only twelve and them thirteen?" she asked sharply.

"Because I gave you a dozen good ears and there were worms in some of theirs," I answered in a conciliatory manner.

"Well, then," she snapped, "I want a worm too!"

I meekly found a wormy ear and stuffed it in her bag.

To live off a garden, you practically have to live in it.
— Frank McKinney Hubbard

Weed better be careful

When my two-year-old was riding his tricycle one spring day, I caught him pedaling through my neighbor's lovely rock garden, and plants were strewn everywhere!

I grabbed him off his trike and sent him home to his room. Then I surveyed the mess.

I knelt down and started to replant as many flowers as I could.

As I worked it dawned on me that Lionel hadn't been out long enough to have done this amount of damage.

I stopped replanting and rang my neighbor's doorbell.

She greeted me cheerfully and, excusing her appearance, explained she had been weeding her garden all morning.

Older . . . and wiser?

Our friend, who had just turned 60, was doing some spring planting with the help of his 91-year-old father. When the older man began to put up beanpoles in straight lines, the son suggested that stacking them tepee-style was better.

A disagreement arose.

"Dad," our friend finally said, sighing, "this is my garden, and I want to use the tepees."

The father threw down his hoe and stomped off towards the house.

"You kids!" he snorted over his shoulder. "Turn sixty and think that you know everything!"

Random selection

My mother-in-law loves to cook, and my father-in-law loves gardening.

One day she needed an onion and went to the mesh bag he had hung near the back door to get one.

They both found the resultant dish tasty — but different. The next morning, as he reached for the mesh bag, Dad announced that he had better plant those tulip bulbs before it rained.

Note: Do not try this at home unless you relish tummy aches.

Heated competition

Strolling past old-world gardens in Nanaimo, British Columbia, I stopped to chat with an elderly man tending his rose bushes.

"I won first prize in our garden-club competition last year," he said.

Without rancor, he added, "I can't enter this year because I'm president. But I will again next year."

I congratulated him, and said I was sure he'd win again with such beautiful roses. "How many members do you compete against?" I asked.

"Just my friend next door. We take turns being president."

It's reaching for the remote right now

Mother has a green thumb. Although some of her growing methods may seem unorthodox, my father has become accustomed to the unusual.

One afternoon she placed an aloe plant on the floor in front of the television set, where it would be in the direct path of a beam of sunshine.

When Dad came into the room he headed straight for the TV. Seeing the aloe plant, he said matter-of-factly, "Sure hope it likes baseball."

Show a little compassion

Some people are said to have a green thumb, but I'm not one of them. In my keeping, plants wither and die.

Yet, I cannot resist the lure of a plant shop, and once inside, I usually discount my past failures and cart home another healthy, thriving victim.

Recently, as I was standing outside a plant shop, gazing with longing through the window at a leafy Dieffenbachia, I felt a hand on my shoulder and heard my husband whisper, "Let it live, dear."

Mark this

My mother, whose talents do not include gardening, was planting seeds one afternoon when I dropped by to visit.

As I gazed at her not-too-straight rows, I suggested that she mark each row so that she would know what she had planted.

Without hesitation she replied, “My dear girl, this is a garden, not a cemetery. I expect all of these seeds to come up and identify themselves.”

A little kindness

Each morning as I walked to work, I would stop for a while at the garden of a big house and chat with the old gardener. He would pick a flower for me, and I would share some goodies from my lunch bag with him.

We fast became good friends, and I told him of my hopes and aspirations. He suggested that I apply for a job with the nearby P.L. Robertson factory. The pay would be better there than what I was making, he assured me.

I told him he should do the same, so we both agreed to apply on the same day.

On that day, while I was filling in my application form, the old gardener walked in. Much to my surprise the office staff stood up and said in unison, “Good morning, P.L.”

I was hired.

Our little secret

It was such a beautiful spring like day that I went out in my yard to do some gardening. I saw my next-door neighbor busily planting rose bushes and walked over to tell her that she would have better luck if she waited a few weeks.

But before I could say anything, she placed her forefinger on her lips.

As we walked back into my yard, she whispered, "I know it's a little early and you know it's a little early, but I don't think the roses know."

You have questions, we have answers

My umbrella plant had grown to the ceiling of my living room.

Not being a gardener, I didn't know what would happen if I cut off the top, so I decided to phone a government horticulturist for expert advice.

"What would happen if I cut off the top of my umbrella plant?" I asked.

"You would have a shorter plant," came the reply.

G.O.A.T.

We own and operate a goat dairy, and every spring brings an influx of city visitors to see the kids.

We had just taken time from our chores one afternoon to show some new arrivals to an interested couple. One very agile goat shot out of the gate, leaped with all four feet into the air, twisted sideways, and then bounded stiff-legged across our freshly planted garden.

"Oh, look!" shouted the woman with delight. "He's gamboling!"

"Yeah," growled my husband in hot pursuit. "With his life!"

Give the customers what they want

The manager of the garden center overhears one of his nurserymen talking to a customer.

"No, we haven't had any in months," says the nurseryman. "And I have no idea when we'll be getting any more."

The customer leaves and the manager strides over. "Never tell a customer we can't get them something," he scolds. "Whatever they want we can always order and deliver it. Understand?"

The nurseryman nods.

"So what did he want?" the manager asks.

"Rain."

GARDENING
America's favorite exercise . . .
and you get a ZUCCHINI!
Quippery

OF SQUIRRELS AND COFFEE BEANS

"A Scientific Explanation of Why It's Not Our Fault That the Neighborhood Squirrels Started Eating Coffee Beans"

by Prisca Bejjani

Day 1.

Dear Neighborhood,

We just wanted to let you know that the potentially erratic behavior of the neighborhood squirrels is completely unrelated to our having dumped a bag of coffee beans in our compost. It was a low-quality brand presented to us from our in-laws, but, being the environmentally conscious people we are, we are composting instead of trashing them.

Day 2.

Dear Neighborhood,

We have hypothesized extensively on the existence of a rare plant that only flowers once every 732 lunar years, and that nocturnally. This plant is assumed to have the propensities to make squirrels run around and around in circles when its perfume is inhaled, as well as causing them to perform acrobatic exercises upon phone lines. No scientific link has been established between imbibing coffee beans by climbing rodents and these performances.

Day 3.

Dear Neighborhood,

We will be delivering lectures on our research in local schools, and hope that we can count on your support. Most parents at the schools have not seen the scratches on cars and the roof shingles torn off in our neighborhood. We greatly appreciate your assistance by silence.

Day 4.

Dear Neighborhood,

We would like to inform you that we will be out of town for the next week and a half, and perhaps permanently, having been awarded an honorary degree from Harvard due to our discoveries. Our permanent absence has nothing to do with being woken up multiple times a night by small chattering mammals, nor with my wife's having been ambushed by squirrels jumping on her hat every time she leaves the house. We also need to rewrite curriculum for all grade levels to include our discoveries.

N.B. No squirrels were harmed in the writing of this article.

DID YOU JUST BUD DIAL ME?
MARK PARISI
©2019 Mark Parisi Dist by Andrews McMeel Synd.
offthemark.com

NATURAL LAWS OF GARDENING

Day follows night. Spring follows winter. Death follows taxes. Everywhere we find underlying, immutable cycles.

Gardeners have distilled these classic patterns and cycles over generations of observation.

- "Annuals" mean disappointment once a year.
- The only way to ensure rain is to give your garden a good soaking.
- Weeds grow at precisely the rate you pull them out.
- Autumn follows summer, winter follows autumn, drought follows planting.
- The only way to guarantee year-round color is to buy a garden gnome.
- No matter how bare your lawn, grass will appear in your garden and in the cracks between paving stones.
- Evergreens go a despondent shade of brown in the winter.
- As ye sow, so shall ye reap, unless you are an amateur gardener.

- Any self-respecting rock will break at least one shovel before accepting its new home.
- When all the chores are done, the avid gardener invents new ones.

Every man reaps what he sows in this life — except the amateur gardener.

— Lesley Hall

Always . . .

The gardening tool you need right now is *always* at the back of the shed.

Never . . .

A man should *never* plant a garden larger than his wife can take care of.

— T.H. Everett

Always . . .

Your lawn is *always* slightly bigger than your will to mow it.

Always . . .

A good gardener *always* plants in threes. One for the bugs, one for the weather, and one for herself.

Never . . .

Your actual plants *never* look like the pictures on the seed packets.

Always . . .

A tomato in the hand is *always* worth two on the vine.

And from gardening humorist Texas Bix Bender . . .

The way to a green thumb is through dirty fingernails.

The fastest-growing thing in your garden is an okra pod or a zucchini you thought was not quite big enough to pick yesterday.

A garden expert is any ordinary person talking about somebody else's garden.

— *Don't Throw in the Trowel*

Plant-based burger
found in the wild
Before harvesting

SEED PACKETS WE'D LIKE TO SEE

De Ree
Lettuce Little Gem
Spring Onion White Lisbon
Beetroot Boltardy
Tomato Moneymaker
Seed Collections
Salad Collection
These don't grow so well for us.

SINCE 1856
FERRY~MORSE
BEAN GARDEN
Kentucky Wonder, Rust Resistant (Pole)
Excellent Pole Bean • Days to Harvest 66
VEGETABLE
Disclaimer: This picture was Photoshopped.

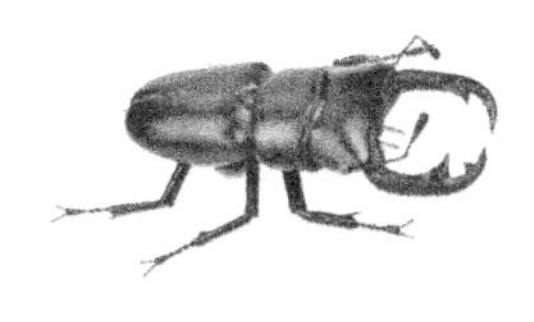

VERDURA
VEGETABLE
BURPEE.
Signature
EGGPLANT
Black Knight
BERENJENA Black Knight
Dark Purple Fruits
FULL SUN
75 DAYS TO MATURITY
Note - Not that many people like eggplant.

HIERBA
HERB
BURPEE.
LAVENDER, MUNSTEAD
Lavandula angustifolia
LAVANDA MUNSTEAD Lavandula angustifolia
Classic Fragrance
FULL SUN
18" HEIGHT
Please try your best not to kill these.

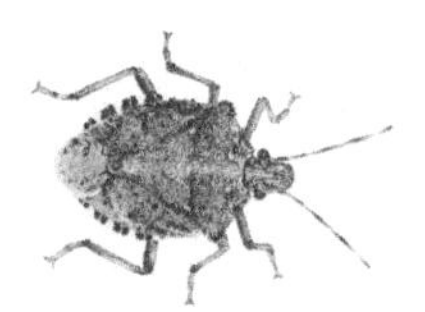

ANUAL
ANNUAL
BURPEE.
Signature
FOUR O' CLOCKS
Marbles Mix
DONDIEGOS Marbles Mix
Drought Tolerant
FULL SUN
20-30" HEIGHT
Honestly, is gardening that much fun?

SINCE 1856
FERRY~MORSE®
WATERMELON
Crimson Sweet
Tasty, Sweet Slices • Days to Harvest 85
VEGETABLE
Alert: Melons attract raccoons.

ORGANIC
Johnsons™
Squash (WINTER) EARLY BUTTERNUT
Organically grown seed, early maturing variety
Will not grow in YOUR plant hardiness zone.
Sow: Mar-May | Harvest: Jul-Oct

De Ree
Lettuce
All Year Round
Customers: You're better off buying lettuce at the supermarket.

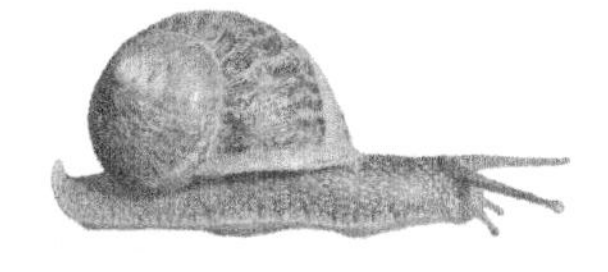

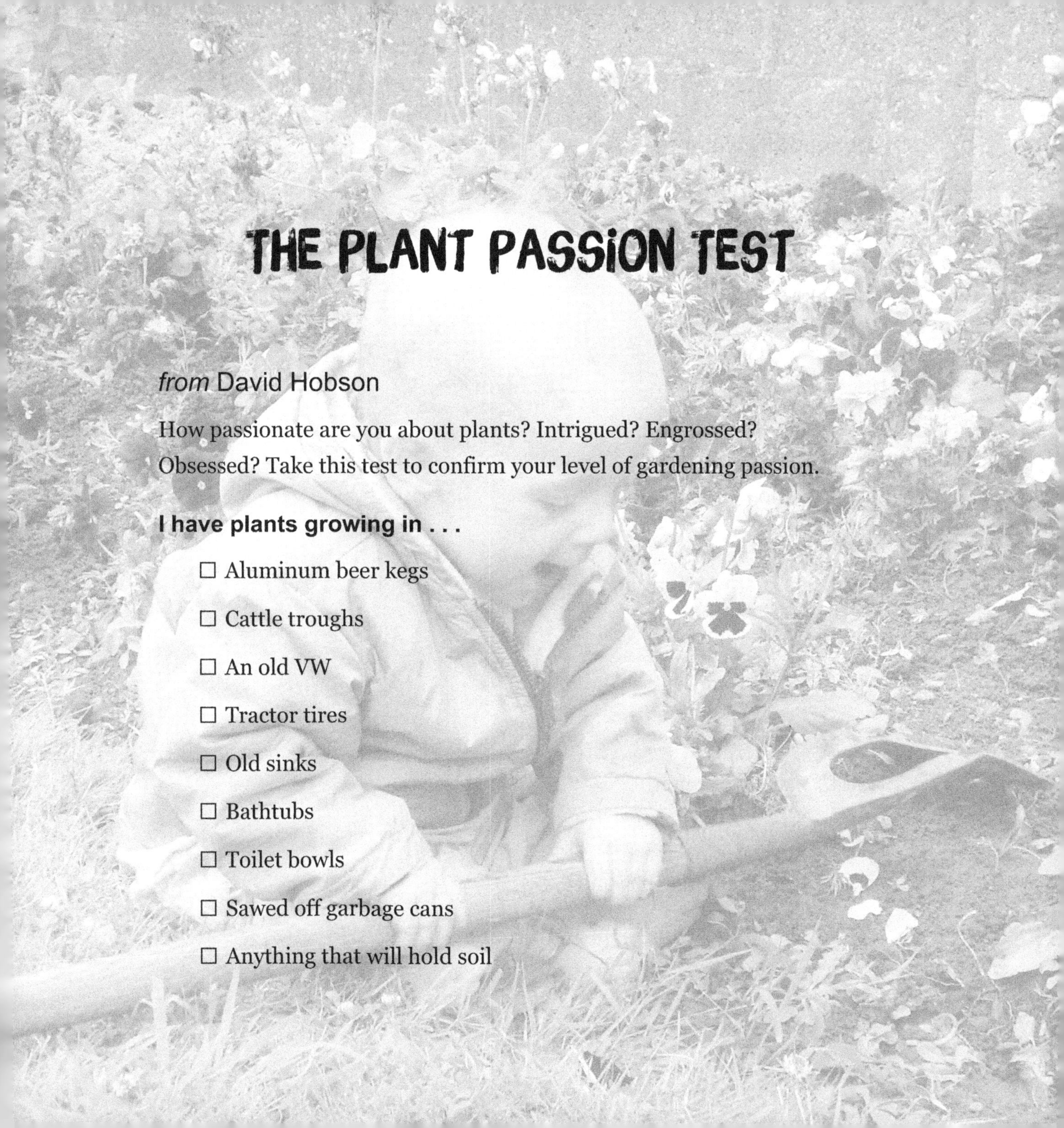

THE PLANT PASSION TEST

from David Hobson

How passionate are you about plants? Intrigued? Engrossed? Obsessed? Take this test to confirm your level of gardening passion.

I have plants growing in . . .

- ☐ Aluminum beer kegs
- ☐ Cattle troughs
- ☐ An old VW
- ☐ Tractor tires
- ☐ Old sinks
- ☐ Bathtubs
- ☐ Toilet bowls
- ☐ Sawed off garbage cans
- ☐ Anything that will hold soil

My monthly water bill is . . .

- ☐ Less than $10
- ☐ $10 to 20
- ☐ $20 to 50
- ☐ $50 plus
- ☐ Unopened
- ☐ Trashed
- ☐ $400 and probation

I choose plants because . . .

- ☐ Of their color
- ☐ Their condition
- ☐ Their size
- ☐ Value for money
- ☐ I had to have it
- ☐ Martha Stewart has one
- ☐ They were giving them away

☐ I can always find room for another

☐ Just because

My friends and family say I'm . . .

☐ A hobby gardener

☐ An enthusiast

☐ A real keener

☐ Nuts about gardening

☐ Obsessive compulsive

☐ A little odd

☐ Harmless, but keep the gate open when visiting

I have moved a new shrub or plant . . .

☐ Once

☐ Twice

☐ Three times

☐ Four times

☐ More times

☐ Still moving it

☐ Stopped taking them from container

I have rescued seeds from . . .

☐ Friends' gardens

☐ Neighbors' gardens

☐ Relatives' gardens

☐ Public gardens

☐ Botanical gardens

☐ Nurseries

☐ Cemeteries

☐ All of the above

I'm usually in the garden . . .

☐ Once a day

☐ Twice a day

☐ All morning

☐ All afternoon

- ☐ Morning and afternoon
- ☐ What's time?
- ☐ I eat there
- ☐ I sleep there
- ☐ Until they stop calling me
- ☐ "Want" me? Find me!

I talk to my plants . . .

- ☐ Once in a while
- ☐ Daily
- ☐ When there's no one around
- ☐ All the time
- ☐ More than I talk to my spouse
- ☐ And my pond fish
- ☐ I leave a cell phone in the garden and call them
- ☐ And I sometimes curse them
- ☐ And they talk to me, don't you know?

You can take this test online at David Hobson's Garden Humour website, home.golden.net/~dhobson/madsoc.htm. "Pass the test," he says, "and on application you will receive an authentic personalized certificate of membership in the world's first cyber garden club for committed gardeners (or gardeners that should be committed)."

An Olympic gold for gardening?

I now believe that gardening is just as grueling as any sport. Why, maybe gardening should be in the Olympics. That would be so thrilling. Can you imagine the spine-tingling tension of a topiary competition, or the excitement of competitive weeding? And let's not forget the sheer titillation of questionable garden clothing.

But then I suppose there'd be the usual scandal over the use of illegal growth hormones (that will be a biggie, I'm sure), and we'd have to watch those hokey interviews with the medalists: "I owe it all to my pony, Jenny, for providing me with what it takes to grow healthy plants." Meanwhile the medalists will all be sitting there holding shovels with trademarks showing and wearing shrink-wrapped spandex with the logos of huge fertilizer companies plastered over them.

— David Hobson, *Diary of a Mad Gardener*

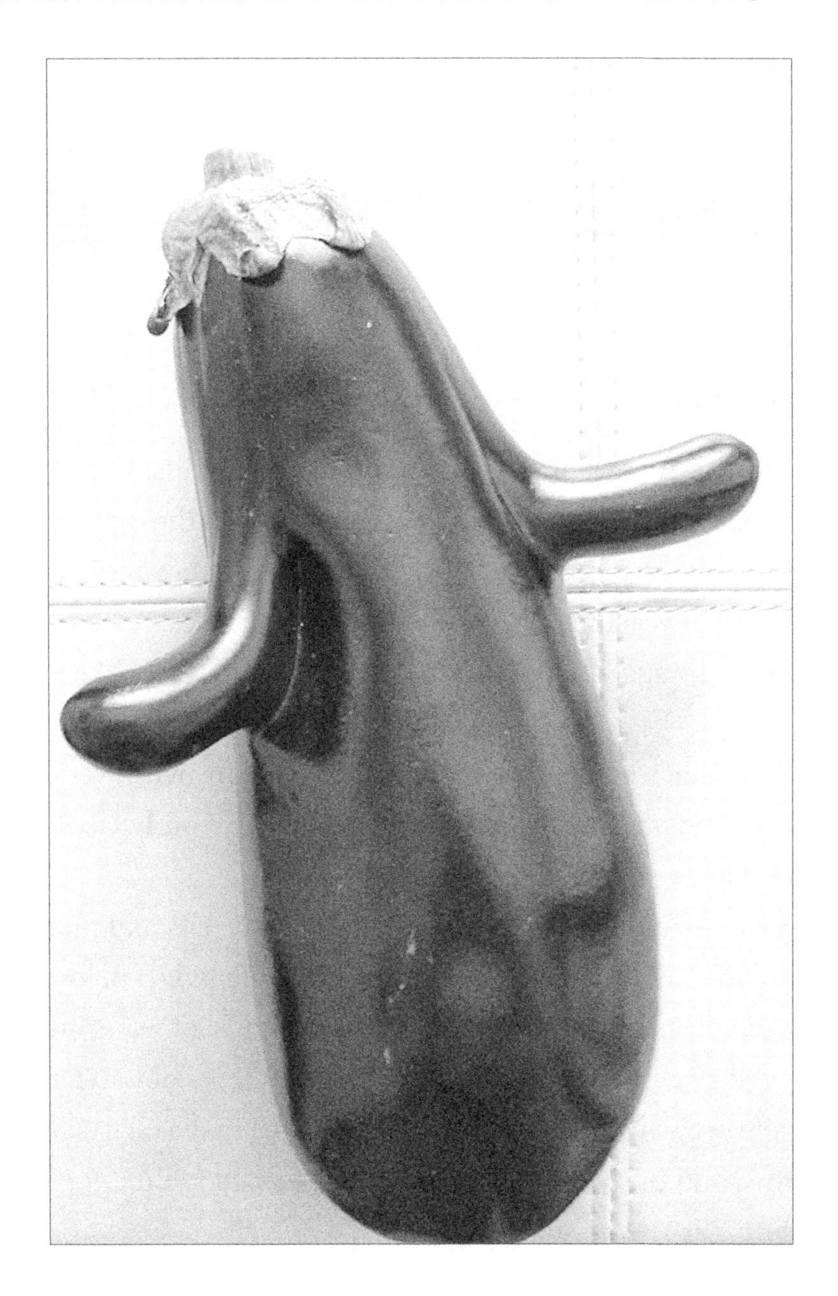

GARDENING WITH YOUR KIDS

by Kate Whinehall

I was planning to write a post about gardening with kids. Everyone's writing them. They write about the joys of digging in the dirt with their kids and seeing the smiles on their faces when they bite into that first home-grown vegetable the child raised themselves.

But then I thought about it and realized, I don't really like gardening with my kids.

You'd think as a homeschooling mom that I'd be overjoyed to incorporate living off the land into our curriculum. And I was. Until we actually tried it.

One early spring day I decided to pull out my seeds and plant a few in peat pots to prepare for the summer. I thought, the kids will love this. I'll teach them about plant propagation, the importance of watering seedlings, and giving the plants enough light and nutrients. They'll watch the entire life cycle from seed to our bellies. We'll make charts and draw pictures and this will be our entire science curriculum for half a year. It'll be great!

Nope.

This is how it went.

I carefully laid newspaper down on the floor, but kids are kind of messy. Did you know that? Before we even got the seeds out, soil was all over the basement. My kids looked like Mike Rowe from Dirty Jobs. It wasn't fun . . . for me.

So, when the weather warmed up, I tried again, outside.

I gave my, then four-year-old, daughter a shovel and showed her where to dig in my square foot garden. I came back a few minutes later and all the soil was outside the garden, on the grass!

So then I thought, forget the digging, I'll just let them plant the seeds. So they picked out sunflower seeds and we planted those in separate pots. The biggest mistake I made was, of course, not labeling the pots. Not with the tag "sunflower," which I did, but with each of my kids' names. Because here's what happens when you forget to label with your kids' names:

Kid 1: You watered my sunflower! MOM! He watered my sunflower! That's MY sunflower!

Kid 2: No. This is MY sunflower. See, your pot had a chip in it.

Kid 1: No it didn't! YOUR pot had a chip! That's my pot!

Kid 2: No, it's not.

Me: (squeezes bridge of nose)

Kid 1: YES, IT IS! (kicks watering can over)

Kid 2: (laughs at the drama of the kicked can)

Kid 1: (screams loudly enough for neighbors 60 houses away to hear)

And that's when I quit and decided I don't really like gardening with my kids.

Plumb right

My daughter Bonnie knew how much I loved flowers, and when she was nine years old, she felt justified taking some branches from our neighbor's blossoming fruit tree.

Realizing where she had got them, but recognizing her intention to please me, I didn't scold her but chose a different approach.

"These are lovely, Bonnie," I said, "but do you realize that if you had left them on the tree, each of these blossoms would have become a cherry?"

"No, they wouldn't have," she stated firmly.

"Oh, yes, they would have. Each of these blossoms would have grown into a cherry."

"No, they wouldn't," she said again stubbornly.

"Bonnie," I said, somewhat angrily, "each one of these blossoms would have become a cherry!"

"Well, okay," she finally conceded, "but they were plums last year!"

Young primates, otherwise known as children, are the single biggest pest in the garden.

— Ivor Grump, *The Grumpy Gardener's Handbook*

COMMUNING WITH YOUR PLANTS

julio torres ~*
@juliothesquare

I started talking to my plants because I heard it's good for them but that has only resulted in the most PAINFUL smalltalk, this morning I was like "Hi... so, you're growing! That's great. That's great. Alright, well, yeah..."

suze orman impersonator
@fired4horney

Replying to @juliothesquare

Sometimes plants take a little while. I thought my mint was a real boring bitch but it turns out she's just shy, now she's my biggest supporter. My lavender is more emotionally needy, I help him. My oregano is a stone cold binch who's too sassy

Replying to @juliothesquare

Read to them some Borges, I hear sunlight/lite surrealism pair nicely

Replying to @juliothesquare

I heard if you pour a little alcohol in the soil they're better conversationalists

You may be a plant whisperer if . . .

- You start talking to your plants . . . and then to your weeds
- You talk to your plants and weeds more than you do to other people
- Your plants and weeds start talking back to you
- You share your innermost thoughts, your secret fears and longings, your hopes and aspirations, your challenges with your partner
- You act on their suggestions
- You act on their stock tips

C'MON, ALREADY!
YO! LADY!
OH, SURE... JUST TAKE YOUR SWEEEET TIME...
HEY! WE'RE THIRSTY OVER HERE!
DARN IMPATIENS...
MARK PARISI
offthemark.com
ATLANTIC FEATURE © 1994 MARK PARISI

YOU'VE BEEN GARDENING TOO LONG WHEN . . .

- You have framed photos of your zucchini and tomatoes on your desk at the office — also in your wallet, which you pull out and show your friends at every chance.
- Your dream of an entertaining Saturday night is wiping the leaves of your plants with soapy water to get rid of aphids.
- You go into your garden when you get home from work — before going inside to see your family.
- You feel a warm inner glow when you gaze at your compost pile.
- You know the weeds in your garden by their Latin names.
- You get robo calls from garden supply corporations.
- You visit friends and can't resist weeding *their* gardens.
- You wake up in the morning having just had a pleasant dream about

dried manure.

- Your garden is tidier than your living room.
- You correct the garden center staff when they give misinformation to customers.
- Your dream vacation is spending a full week in your garden.
- You switch from Rogaine to Miracle Gro.
- You sneer at gardeners who don't start annuals from seed.
- You install exterior cameras so you can look at your garden when you're away.
- You start adding liquid kelp fertilizer to your smoothies.
- You install a security system in your garden but not your house.
- You rent a truck and drive half a day to get a good deal on 500 pounds of aged manure.
- Your kids groan when you make an unplanned stop at a garden center.
- You converse with your plants more than with your family and friends.
- You keep your jar of powdered rooting hormone on the same shelf as your vitamins.
- Your gardening friends consult you on how to make their own powdered rooting hormone.

- Your partner gives you a new tumbling composter for your birthday and you can't imagine a more thoughtful or romantic gift.
- You plan your vacations around planting times.

- You keep a small auxiliary supply of garden soil under your fingernails.
- Your shed has become your second home.
- You let unrecognized volunteers grow just to see if it is something you could use.
- You haven't been to your favorite garden center for a few days and they call you at home to make sure you're OK.
- You include frogs, toads, and lizards among your best friends.

- You squash invasive bugs by hand without a second thought.
- You don't mind when the 40-pound bag of topsoil that you put on your back seat (because it wouldn't fit in your trunk along with all the other bags) splits because what are cars for other than to haul topsoil?
- You interpret *multiculturalism* to mean planting flowers among your vegetable beds.
- You name your kids Rose, Daisy, and Violet — and one of them is a boy.
- You wake up at 2:30 a.m. to jot down your sudden thought about where you want to move plants.
- You've been known to dumpster dive when you open the lid and spot a plant you can rescue or material you can compost.
- You hold memorial services in your garden after an early killing frost.
- You've taken an obsessive interest in groundcover.
- You use your Fitbit to track your heart rate and the number of steps you take around your garden.
- Your selfies always include your garden.
- You buy plants on clearance — even when you have no idea where you'll put them.

GANGRENE THUMBS

I have no plants in my house. They won't live for me. Some of them don't even wait to die, they commit suicide.

— Jerry Seinfeld

I've killed so many plants. I walked into a nursery once and my face was on a wanted poster.

— Rita Rudner

I do not have a green thumb. I can't even get mold to grow on last month's takeout.

— Johnnye Jones Gibson

I consider every plant hardy until I have killed it myself.

— Peter Smithers, botanist and British diplomat

I belong to Gardeners Anonymous. Whenever I feel the urge to break the soil, I call a number and a horticulturist rushes over to tie me to the trellis. You see, I have a black thumb. I'm an Israeli in reverse: I turn gardens into deserts.

— Michael Feldman, *Whad'ya Know?*

Can't even get compost to rot . . .

My ability to produce compost efficiently is way up there with my ability to attract nesting birds. What happens when I put leaves or grass into a compost bin would surely interest scientists.

Nothing happens at all. No decomposition takes place whatsoever. It's like the moment plant matter goes in through the top everything becomes cryogenically frozen.

— Ivor Grump, *The Grumpy Gardener's Handbook*

I have a rock garden. Last week three of them died.
— Richard Diran

Take my wife . . . please

Now if you thought I was a bad gardener, my ineptitude and lack of ability pales into insignificance when it comes to my wife's treatment of house plants. When unsuspecting house plants get dragged back to our house in the back of her car, they don't see the outline of a suburban house, they see the outline of the Bates Motel accompanied by that screeching violin sound effect.

The reason for this is her bizarre watering regime. She employs what is known as the desert/mangrove technique for watering. The first stage of this is to forget to water the new houseplant for a couple of weeks so that the leaves begin to wilt and the compost dries up. This is known as the desert phase.

After that there is a sudden guilty rush to give it lots of water all the time . . . which rushes straight out the bottom of the plant pot. This is known as the mangrove phase. Similar to a tidal mangrove swamp, the water comes in, and goes out again, comes in, and goes out again.

This is the pattern of treatment until the plant is thoroughly exhausted and gives up the ghost.

— Ivor Grump, *The Grumpy Gardener's Handbook*

Nothing works . . .

One year I planted potatoes and forgot where. Another time, I had a vigorous tomato plant, but it was on the compost heap. For three months I gave succor to a weed impersonating rhubarb. I tried planting fish, like the Indians, but none grew. Sowing naked by the light of the full moon proved to be of no avail; the neighbors merely moved their patio parties indoors.

— Jeannie Dietz

Ellen's sure-fire technique

To be honest, I'd be the last person who should be doling out gardening advice. I don't have the patience for growing things. Yes, I realize there's nothing quite as satisfying as eating food that you've pulled up from the ground and that's why, at the height of the planting season, I bury cans of tomato soup in my backyard and dig them up again in late spring.

— Ellen DeGeneres, *The Funny Thing Is . . .*

"You're not stretching yourself as a gardener if you're not killing plants."
— J.C. Raulstong

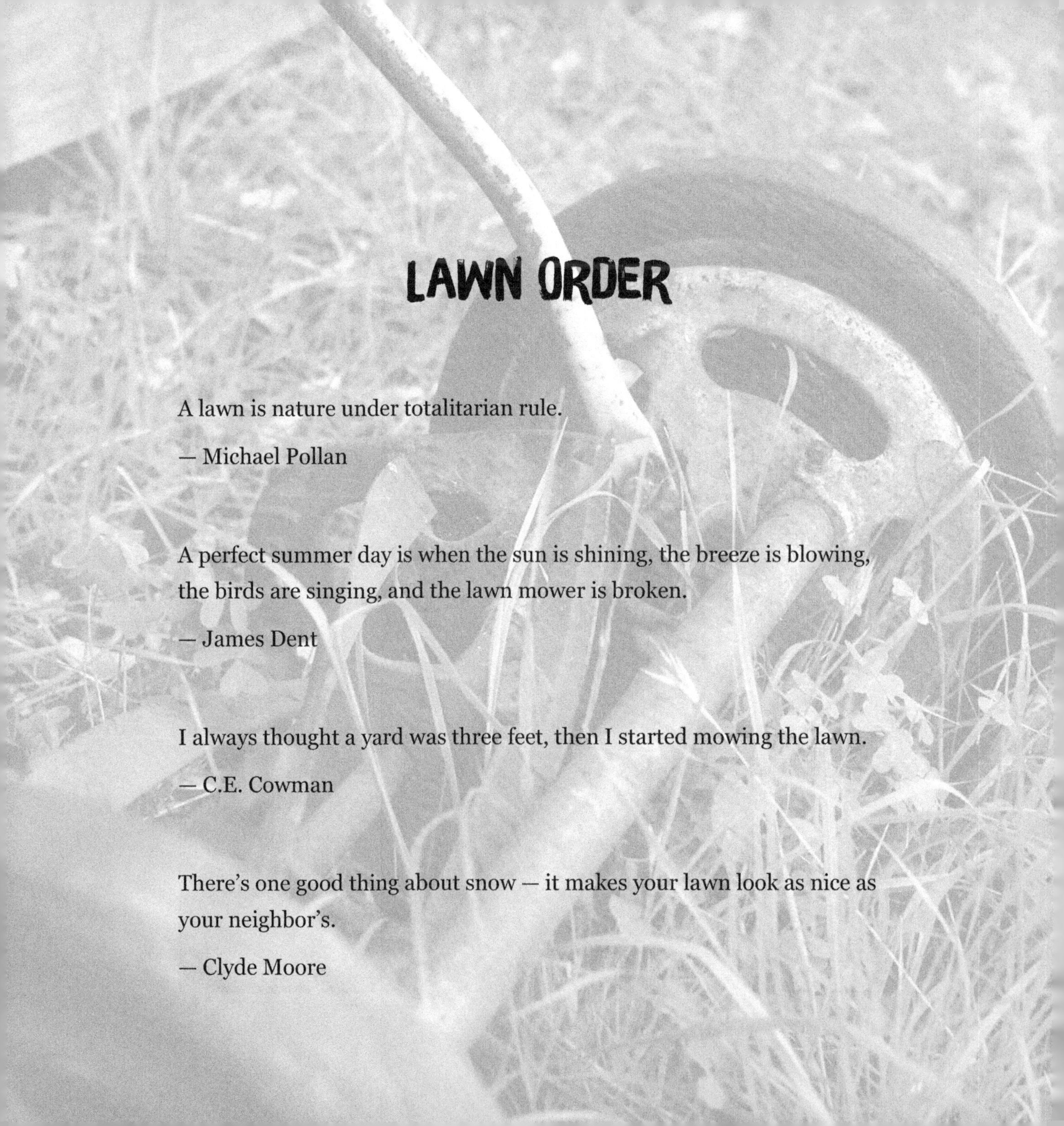

LAWN ORDER

A lawn is nature under totalitarian rule.

— Michael Pollan

A perfect summer day is when the sun is shining, the breeze is blowing, the birds are singing, and the lawn mower is broken.

— James Dent

I always thought a yard was three feet, then I started mowing the lawn.

— C.E. Cowman

There's one good thing about snow — it makes your lawn look as nice as your neighbor's.

— Clyde Moore

from The Onion

NEWS IN BRIEF

Dad Busy Throwing Seeds Or Something On Lawn

WARRENSBURG, MO — Speculating that it's probably meant to make the grass greener or fuller or something, living room sources reported Thursday that local dad Brian Winfield, 45, is currently busy throwing little seeds of some kind all over the front lawn. "He's been at it for a few hours now," said Megan Winfield, 15, who confirmed that her father is carrying a large bag around, grabbing handfuls of small grain-like kernels, and dropping them methodically on the grass. "He got up really early to do this, so apparently it's important. He does it every year." At press time, Winfield was reportedly standing at the edge of the lawn, wiping the sweat from his brow and admiring whatever it was he had just done.

Nothing says "This is someone else's problem now" quite like a leaf blower.

— Unknown

Grass is the cheapest plant to install and the most expensive to maintain.

— Pat Howell

I appreciate the misunderstanding I have had with Nature over my perennial border. I think it is a flower garden; she thinks it is a meadow lacking grass — and tries to correct the error.

—Sara Stein

How to determine the proper height to cut your grass

- Measure the height of your neighbor's grass after it has just been cut.
- Cut your grass 1/4 inch shorter.

The rain finally stopped —
now Dad can cut the grass!

from The Onion

NEWS

Republicans Back Universal Lawn-Care Bill

WASHINGTON, DC — Seeking to make "comprehensive, high-quality lawn and garden care accessible to all Americans," a coalition of House Republicans Monday introduced H.R. 4702, the Hastert-Armey Lawn-Care Reform Act.

"A healthy, productive, green lawn should be a reality for everyone, not just the rich," said Sen. Dick Armey (R-TX), co-author of the bill. "No American should be forced to endure crabgrass, uneven edges, and poorly aerated soil just because they can't afford a good landscaper."

Under the bill, states would be given financial incentives to provide residents with well-manicured lawns of uniform length. Working with designated local lawn-care providers, states would also subsidize turf-building, leaf-blowing, and hedge-trimming services — making allowances for fertilizer and decorative-bark deductibles — for residents earning less than $48,500 a year.

"It's time we took the reins of power from greedy, uncaring neighborhood associations, who all too often force the private citizen to shoulder much of the financial burden of caring for their lawns," Rep. Paul Ryan (R-WI) said. "How sad it is that we are the richest, most powerful nation on Earth, yet millions of us do not have access to a good herbicide for our broadleaf weeds."

The bill has already received hearty endorsements from several leading suburban environmental groups, as well as grass-roots support from those living in nitrogen-poor areas.

"No longer will you or your neighbor have to live with discolored turf, dead spots, and inadequately pruned shrubs," Armey said. "From now on, all Americans, regardless of how soft their soil is, will enjoy the right to quality weeding, mowing, and irrigation. This bill will give each and every lawn the tender, loving care it deserves."

Though Democratic critics argue that the establishment of a federal lawn-care system would increase administrative costs while depriving the individual of his choice of lawn-care providers, most are willing to support the bill in principle.

"The bill, as proposed, is not without flaws," Sen. Paul Wellstone (D-MN) said. "As it stands, it will benefit John Deere, Scott's, and the other companies that make up Big Lawn as much as it does the average homeowner. But it is undeniably a step in the right direction."

If passed, the bill would provide full fertilizer coverage for the estimated 22 million U.S. lawns that are currently uncovered.

"We cannot afford to take the health of our nation's lawns for granted," Armey said. "But for every problem, I have full confidence that American landscaping know-how can find a solution, whether it be hardy perennial grasses, dwarf shade trees, or even full-scale resodding. We will find a solution, because we must. After all, what is more important than having a nice lawn?"

GARDENING
Loam Sweet Loam!

from The Onion

NEWS IN BRIEF

Dad Can't Believe Lawn Didn't Get Him Anything for Father's Day

WINCHESTER, VA — Telling reporters that he can't help but feel a little hurt, 52-year-old local father Trevor Jackson expressed his surprise and disappointment Sunday that his lawn didn't bother to get him anything for Father's Day this year. "It's not like I expect a big production on Father's Day or anything, but I guess I thought my lawn would get me some sort of little present — a card, at the very least," said Jackson, adding that as the day went on, he slowly realized he wouldn't be receiving any kind of gift at all from the grass in his front yard. "I care for it, I buy it anything it needs, I spend every weekend with it, and on the one day that's supposed to be about me, I don't even get so much as a 'Happy Father's Day' greeting. I mean, would it kill my lawn to show me just a little appreciation once a year?" Despite his initial frustration, Jackson later confirmed that taking care of his lawn is its own reward, and he was happy to simply have a quiet Sunday afternoon together with the patch of fertilized grass.

Where is the grass always greener?

The grass is always greener where you water it.

The grass is always greener over the septic tank.

— Erma Bombeck

I just finished mowing the lawn.

ATLANTIC FEATURE © 2002 MARK PARISI
offthemark.com
MARK PARISI
MARTA'S YOGA CLASSES START TO PAY OFF

LAWNS, ST. FRANCIS, AND GOD

GOD – St. Francis, you know all about gardens and nature. What in the world is going on down there in the USA? What happened to the dandelions, violets, thistle and stuff I started eons ago? I had a perfect, no-maintenance garden plan. Those plants grow in any type of soil, withstand drought and multiply with abandon. The nectar from the long lasting blossoms attracts butterflies, honeybees and flocks of songbirds. I expected to see a vast garden of colors by now. But all I see are these green rectangles.

ST. FRANCIS – It's the tribes that settled there, Lord. The Suburbanites. They started calling your flowers weeds and went to great lengths to kill them and replace them with grass.

GOD – Grass? But it's so boring. It's not colorful. It doesn't attract butterflies, birds, and bees, only grubs and sod worms. It's temperamental with temperatures. Do these Suburbanites really want all that grass growing there?

ST. FRANCIS – Apparently so, Lord. They go to great pains to grow it and keep it green. They begin each spring by fertilizing grass and poisoning any other plant that crops up in the lawn.

GOD – The spring rains and warm weather probably make grass grow really fast. That must make the Suburbanites happy.

ST. FRANCIS – Apparently not, Lord. As soon as it grows a little, they cut it, sometimes twice a week.

GOD – They cut it? Do they then bale it like hay?

ST. FRANCIS – Not exactly Lord. Most of them rake it up and put it in bags.

GOD – They bag it? Why? Is it a cash crop? Do they sell it?

ST. FRANCIS – No, sir — just the opposite. They pay to throw it away.

GOD – Now, let me get this straight. They fertilize grass so it will grow. And when it does grow, they cut it off and pay to throw it away?

ST. FRANCIS – Yes, sir.

GOD – These Suburbanites must be relieved in the summer when we cut back on the rain and turn up the heat. That surely slows the growth and saves them a lot of work.

ST. FRANCIS – You aren't going to believe this, Lord. When the grass stops growing so fast, they drag out hoses and pay more money to water it so they can continue to mow it and pay to get rid of it.

GOD – What nonsense. At least they kept some of the trees. That was a sheer stroke of genius if I do say so myself. The trees grow leaves in the spring to provide beauty and shade in the summer. In the autumn they fall to the ground and form a natural blanket to keep moisture in the soil and protect the trees and bushes. Plus, as they rot, the leaves form compost to enhance the soil. It's a natural circle of life.

ST. FRANCIS – You'd better sit down, Lord. The Suburbanites have drawn a new circle. As soon as the leaves fall, they rake them into great piles and pay to have them hauled away.

GOD – No. What do they do to protect the shrub and tree roots in the winter and to keep the soil moist and loose?

ST. FRANCIS – After throwing away the leaves, they go out and buy something which they call mulch. They haul it home and spread it around in place of the leaves.

GOD – And where do they get this mulch?
ST. FRANCIS – They cut down trees and grind them up to make the mulch.

GOD – Enough! I don't want to think about this anymore. St. Catherine, you're in charge of the arts. What movie have you scheduled for us tonight?

ST. CATHERINE – *Dumb and Dumber*, Lord. It's a really stupid movie about. . . .

GOD – Never mind, I think I just heard the whole story from St. Francis.

INSECTS AND OTHER INPESTATIONS

Mosquito: An insect that makes you like flies better.

Crabgrass can grow on bowling balls in airless rooms, and there is no known way to kill it that does not involve nuclear weapons.

— Dave Barry

It may be the "circle of life" and all that baloney, but it gets on my nerves. We all know how ecology works: Plant grows, bug eats plant, bigger bug eats smaller bug, reptile eats bigger bug, mammal eats reptile, man comes out of conservatory shouting angrily at mammal to get out of his ****ing garden.

— Ivor Grump, *The Grumpy Gardener's Handbook*

LET'S GO TO THE OTHER END OF THE LEAF...
ROAD TRIP!
offthemark.com
©2015 Mark Parisi Dist. by Universal UClick
MARK PARISI

A mother found her 2-year-old chewing on a slug. After overcoming a wave of disgust, she said, "Well — what does it taste like?"

The child replied: "Worms."

Where's the after-party?

SLUG
CROSSING

Looks like I'll need ropes to get down to that cuke . . .

The garden's been dug up? That's terrible!
No, I have no idea. . . .
Have you talked to the cat?

GARDENING
IT'S A SLUGFEST!
Quippery

POTTED

connor
@connorfranta

i have cameras in my house that i can watch on an app while im away which is really cool bc i can see all my plants dying slowly in realtime

Kayla Sokol
@Goodenoughperf

Replying to @jonnysun

I just turned 26, I'm going through Some Shit, and I just started collecting plants. They keep dying. I'm not claiming to speak nature yet.

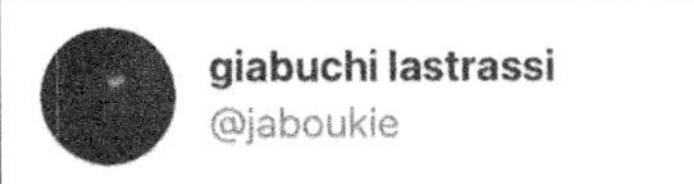

me: *buys aloe vera plant* i'll name you healthcare

Replying to @jonnysun

Me, 15: My friends laughed at me because I didn't want to drink.
Me, 25: My friends died because I forgot to water them.

me, 16: why do ppl own plants lmao
me, 26, filling my empty heart by filling my room w plants: my first language is & always has been Nature

millennial culture is buying a bunch of potted succulents to fulfill your evolutionary desire to care for something during your prime reproductive years

Those tingles you feel walking
into a garden center . . .
That's all your good judgment
exiting your body . . .

Should you buy another plant?

If you can't pot them, boot them!

Going out to get some groceries.

Coming back like:

PHALLIC FUNGUS:

GETTING STINKHORN OUT OF YOUR STINKIN' GARDEN

by Kate Whinehall

We moved to a new house where the yard is heavily mulched with wood chips. It looks really nice, but I don't have much experience with mulch simply because mulch costs money and I'm lazy.

After a few heavy rains I noticed these nasty things growing in our yard.

Ick! That greenish-brown wet-looking area toward the top is indeed wet, and reeks of decaying flesh, therefore attracting flies. Some of these were up to around seven inches long.

After some research (asking my friends on Facebook what this stinky, slimy crap growing in my yard and attracting flies is) I learned that it's a fungus called *Stinkhorn*.

So I googled "Stinkhorn."

I learned that it produces its slimy, stinky substance to attract flies because that's how the spores are spread. See, God does have a sense of humor, but . . . barf.

While deep in research, I noticed that the Latin word for the family of Stinkhorn mushrooms is "Phallaceae," as in "phallic." Yep.

Later, my friend, Julie, added this photo to my "WTH is this crap growing in my yard" Facebook thread.

This mushroom is also found in the Phallaceae family of fungi. The Latin name truly fits.

And, I guess not so ironically, this is the stinkhorn egg when it's cut open.

I'm not making this stuff up.

So obviously I didn't want these things growing in my yard and I definitely didn't want them to spread, as they were doing so quite quickly. So based on my friend Kenya's advice and what I googled on how to get rid of them, I did the following:

Got a plastic trash bag and gloves. They suggested disposable gloves, but I didn't have any, so I wore ski gloves. Just kidding, I wore gardening gloves.

I dug those suckers out, "roots" and all. The "roots" look like small white eggs and there were a lot of them. I kind of felt like a gold miner digging for nuggets of gold, except I hated the freaking gold I found.

I put everything I dug up into a plastic bag.

I tied it up and threw it in the trash, not in the compost bin or with other yard scrap waste, *in the trash*.

Some people recommend boiling water and bleach to get rid of the remaining spores, but I didn't do that because . . . boiling water and bleach.

Then I left my gloves and trowel in the sun to roast all that lingering nasty sporey fungus off.

I've looked back in my garden every day to see if any stinkhorns grew that I had missed. I found a few and dug those up and threw them away. Actually, I just threw them in the middle of my driveway to die and roast because I was too lazy to get a trash bag.

That was last week.

We had another heavy rain two nights ago and wouldn't you know it, those freaking things came back with a vengeance. I dug their little fly-infested, stinking souls out of the ground again. This time, I relented and got the boiling water out along with a trash bag. But, being my lazy self, I just hit one small area with the water and decided to see how the rest goes with just being removed and tossed in the trash – at least I didn't leave them in the middle of the driveway this time.

I went out five minutes ago to check again. I only saw two small Stinkhorns which I quickly removed. And that was all great, but then I found THIS! What the heck are these?!? [See next page . . .]

The battle continues:

GARDENING HAZARDS

The letters of the word GARDEN
can be rearranged to spell *DANGER*

It's well known that gardening is America's most popular pastime. Less well known is how dangerous gardening can be.

HEATSTROKE, SUNSTROKE, STROKE

Signs and symptoms of heatstroke/sunstroke may include:

- Headache
- Feeling desperately thirsty
- Feeling very hot
- Nausea and active vomiting
- The desire to pull just one more weed before going inside . . . and just one more . . . and just one . . .

Won't be gardening tomorrow —
got absolutely baked today!

Even short exposures to direct sun can cause dangerous sunburn. Prolonged exposure can cause human skin to erupt with unsightly sunspots, age spots, moles, melanomas, patches of hair, tattoos, and pieces of metal.

Sun exposure also rapidly ages the skin. There's a simple formula that gardeners use to calculate how old their face and skin will look due to sun exposure if they do not take appropriate precautions: Calculate the number of seasons you spend in your garden, triple it, and add it to your chronological age. So if you're 30 and work for the next 5 years, unprotected, in your garden, then 5 years from now you'll look like you're 50 years old (5x3= 15; 15+35=50).

So to avoid these hazards (including doing the math) it's important to protect yourself against exposure to direct sunlight.

Bear in mind that even the best sunscreens do not provide failsafe protection, and they need to be reapplied at least every few hours. And while keeping your skin covered by clothing is a good idea, it's important to know that harmful rays can also penetrate cloth.

Smart gardening tips for SUN SAFETY

The smart gardener will do each of the following:

- Cover your body with a generous layer of SPF 2000 sunscreen; reapply every 10 minutes.
- Wear clothing sufficient to cover any exposed skin. The heavier the

cloth, the better. We recommend rubberized canvas. Hazmat suits are highly effective.

- Then stay inside and watch TV.

RAKES

Gardeners famously leave rakes on the ground with tines upturned — only to step on the tines in such a way as to lever the rake handle rapidly upward, just like in the cartoons, cracking themselves on the face and forehead.

Or else they will step directly down onto the tines, impaling their feet. When patients arrive at ER with a line of perfectly spaced holes through their feet, the doctors don't even ask how it happened — especially if the patient has dirt under the fingernails.

Smart gardening tips for RAKE SAFETY

- Avoid using rakes.
- If you must use a rake, make sure, when you lay it on the ground, that the tines are facing up — NO, sorry! — facing *down.*
- When you are not using the rake, keep it carefully locked up so children cannot get to it.
- Write your government leaders about passing common sense rake

laws. See the NRA (National Rake Association) website for a summary of proposed laws, supported by a vast majority of Americans.

INSECTS

Chiggers

Contrary to popular belief, chiggers do not lay eggs beneath your skin, which then hatch and grow, feasting on your subcutaneous bodily fluids, laying eggs of their own, which hatch and migrate to different regions of your body, generation after generation, until that species of chigger evolves out of existence, but not before leaving your body a shriveled, fleshless, pock-marked bag of skin.

This is just "suburban legend." The truth is: It's worse.

No, seriously — chigger bites are not fatal. But sometimes you may wish they were.

Smart gardening tips for INSECT SAFETY

- Coat yourself with insect repellent. Do this AFTER you've covered yourself with sunscreen.
- Make sure no areas of skin are exposed.

- To protect against chiggers: Tuck your pants into your socks.
- Don the hazmat suit.
- Then stay inside and watch television

If you DO get a chigger infestation:

- Don't panic.
- Resist the temptation to scratch, claw, or swat the area — use a straitjacket if needed. NEVER signal to chiggers that they've won.
- Most anti-itch medications are useless. We recommend a simple DYI preparation, equal parts aloe vera gel, witch hazel, and concrete mix. Add a few drops of lavender oil, peppermint oil, or eucalyptus oil.

SNAKES

Garter snakes, garden snakes, gardener snakes, and *ribbon snakes* are the types of snakes people commonly find in their gardens.

Garden snakes are described as "virtually" harmless – meaning they can, in certain circumstances, be harmful.

When garden snakes feel threatened, they flash into flight-or-fight mode. When they take flight, they'll often seek the nearest dark space, which can be inside your pants and up your leg. They'll quickly slither as high as they can go, usually reaching the crotch area within seconds.

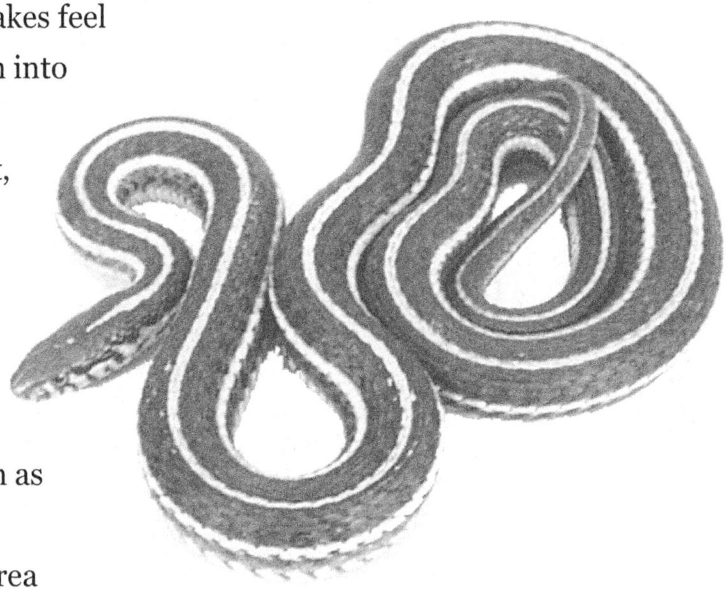

But here, reaching a dead end, unable to move higher and feeling trapped, they may panic further and start to bite at any warm piece of you within reach.

You must remain absolutely motionless. Resist the temptation to wiggle, wriggle, slap, scream, drop trou, or jump in the lake.

After some time — perhaps a few hours, perhaps in the dark hours before dawn — the snake will feel safe enough to move again. Then it will slither its way down your leg and back out into fresh air and freedom. Then, and then only, should you feel free to move.

Snakebites are reported every year in every one of the 48 contiguous states, and if you want to totally avoid poisonous snakes, you'll need to move Alaska or Hawaii, the only states without them.

If your garden is in the Amazon rainforest, you can of course expect to see the occasional green anaconda slithering its 17-foot, 150-pound body among your zucchini, on the hunt for a dog, cat, or child. Do not think you can make it go away by punching it in the nose (that's for sharks), making a ruckus (bears), or staring it in the eyes (uncomfortable first dates).

Smart gardening tips for SNAKE safety

- Avoid working in your garden when snakes are not hibernating.

COMPOST PILES

Standard around many gardens, these can pose grave danger. Heaven forbid you should fall into a compost pile — and it can happen.

Smart gardening tips for COMPOST SAFETY

- Do not allow children to play unsupervised around the compost pile.
- Do not tend the compost pile while under the influence of alcohol, drugs, or anything that impairs mental clarity.
- Be sure to have life rings nearby. Airboats work well for larger compost pile rescues.

If you fall into a compost pile

Please know what to do — ahead of time. The technique is like escaping from quicksand:

- Keep calm.
- If you happen to be holding a rake, a shovel, or a lawnmower, try to use these implements to pull yourself toward "shore."
- If you're in only up to your knees, sit down slowly. If you're up to your

waist, lean back. As with quicksand, you'll sink if you're upright, but float if you're spread out horizontally.

- Now begin to pull your legs out, wiggling them if you need to. Be patient — this can take a while.
- With both legs free, crawl out of the compost pile.
- Quickly hose yourself off with powerful hose stream of water, to dislodge any compost adhering to your body.
- Then call 911, or have someone rush you directly to ER, because the compost pile's decomposing action will have started to go to work on your body. You've seen what it can do to corn cobs and grapefruit peels — it turns them into fine black powder.

It sometimes happens that people who fall into compost piles are not rescued or cannot escape. Tragically, their bodies are entirely consumed.

Therefore, smart gardeners, as part of their wills, leave instructions about where in their gardens they wish this compost to be spread. Usually, they ask to have the compost spread in their own garden.

This is a simple thing to do, and it spares your family members and next of kin the agonizing decision — and potential family-fracturing arguments — about who should get your composted remains or where it should go.

Did you hear about the gardener who fell into a pile of his fertilizer and suffocated? They had to do a compost-mortem.

— from *The Simpsons*

BACK INJURY

One of the most pleasing sounds of springtime to be heard all over the country is the contented cooing of osteopaths as people pick up their garden spades.

— Oliver Pritchett

SPHAGNUM MOSS

Don't even go there.

GROWING UP IS STRESSFUL ENOUGH WITHOUT THESE IDEALIZED BILLBOARDS TO LIVE UP TO...
LILIUM CORSICA
ATLANTIC FEATURE © 2000 MARK PARISI
offthemark.com
MARK PARISI

GARDENING
Embrace your life ...
Get your hands dirty!
Quippery

ZUCCHiNi ZOO

Zucchini to Feed the Masses

by Bud Herron

The Japanese claim — and have claimed for years — that the answer to feeding the ever-increasing world populace is the soybean. Others — the Chinese and the Indians notably among them — say the solution is kelp, a coarse brown seaweed.

My wife, Ann, on the other hand, is a champion of zucchini. She maintains that Bartholomew County alone has enough zucchini to feed all of South America, the Fiji Islands and half of Bavaria. Hawcreek Township by itself has so much zucchini this year that you can hardly walk through Elsbury's Greenhouse without some total stranger jumping out from behind a potted tree and forcing some into your shopping bag. I took Ann to a movie last week and the ticket salesman tried to give me my change from a $20 bill in zucchini.

I'm really not sure where all the zucchini has come from. I don't remember zucchini being around when I was a child growing up in Hope.

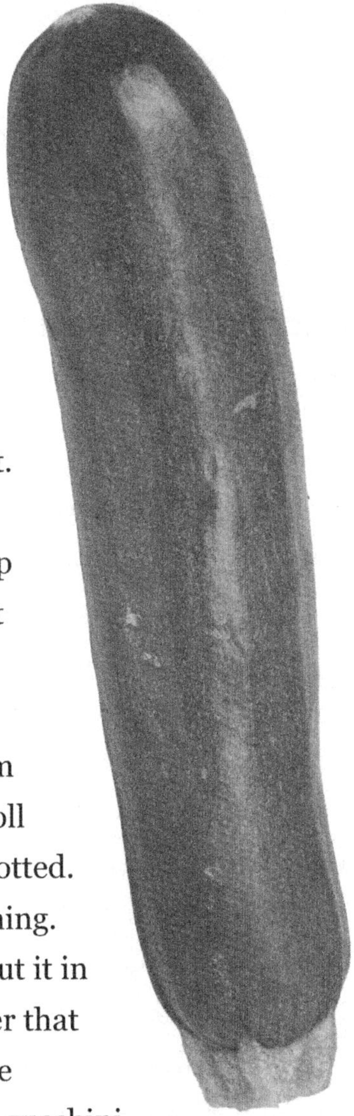

If people grew it, they hid it somewhere — or claimed it was a giant cucumber, or cut it up and concealed it in the fruit salad.

In any case, no one talked about it or ever offered it to anyone. We all ate corn and beans and other vegetables more adequately designed for human consumption. Then about 30 years ago, zucchini started popping up here and there.

At first, no one quite knew what to do with it. My aunt Mabel sliced it and fried it and discovered it tastes like grease. My sister cut it up and baked it in a tuna casserole and found that it tastes like tuna. My uncle Jim tried making zucchini wine and said it tastes like water with a slight kick. The best idea in those days came from my daughter, who dressed up a zucchini like a doll and pushed it around her baby carriage until it rotted.

The fact is, zucchini does not taste like anything. As Ann says, the joy of zucchini is that you can put it in anything and it will take on the flavor of whatever that anything is. Her theory is that when Jesus fed the multitudes with five loaves and two fish, he used zucchini

NATIONAL SNEAK SOME
ZUCCHINI
ONTO YOUR NEIGHBOR'S PORCH DAY
AUGUST 8
48
Zucchini
THE OLD
FARMER'S ALMANAC

filler to stretch the meal enough to make it go around. If you have surprise dinner guests, you simply add zucchini and what was designed to feed four will now feed 12.

This summer Ann has become to zucchini what George Washington Carver was to the peanut. She has served zucchini pizza, zucchini cake, zucchini-apple pie, zucchini lasagna, zucchini soup, zucchini stroganoff, Moo Goo Gai Zucchini, Zucchini Burrito el Grande and Zucchini Bombay with Cherry Sauce. All of that was thoroughly disgusting in appearance but tasted like absolutely nothing except whatever sauce she poured over it.

And, outside of Zucchini Bombay with Cherry Sauce (which I sealed in a plastic bag and hid behind a couch cushion when she went to answer the doorbell), we managed to swallow most of it.

In addition to the endless culinary delights she has created with zucchini, she also says she can make other things from it — such as glue, shoe polish, varnish remover, deodorant soap and anti-depressant suppositories. She currently is working on a method of spinning zucchini into pantyhose.

And a wonderful part of all of this — Ann says — is that the more zucchini you use the more you seem to have. Our entire refrigerator is full. The cabinet tops are full. The freezer is full. Even my work bench in the garage has been taken over by zucchini, blissfully waiting to become a part of some future giant step for humanity.

Meanwhile out in the garden, the plants continue to produce at a rate of about six squash a second and friends and neighbors from around the globe continue to donate more.

Who says the world is doomed to end in the dust of a nuclear mushroom? From my house it appears we may all simply be squashed to death.

The trouble is, you cannot grow just one zucchini. Minutes after you plant a single seed, hundreds of zucchinis will barge out of the ground and sprawl around the garden, menacing the other vegetables. At night, you will be able to hear the ground quake as more and more zucchinis erupt.

— Dave Barry

Last night we had three small zucchinis for dinner that were grown within fifty feet of our back door. I estimate they cost somewhere in the neighborhood of $371.49 each.

— Andy Rooney

Every year, in mid-summer, with no warning, all my friends and neighbors sell their homes, move to undisclosed locations, and change their identities.

Which is sad because that's just when
I'm about to start harvesting zucchinis.

nevona
@nevona
two corgis afraid of large zucchini

Take my
zucchini . . .
Please!

DEFINING TERMS

Every field has its own terminology, and gardening is no exception, where it's important to know the meaning of certain key terms.

Veteran gardeners have an insider's term for the word *terminology*. "You gotta learn the *worminology*," they'll sometimes say to beginners with a wink. Or: "You just starting out? Get a handle on the *verminology*."

Herewith, excerpts from the Seeds & Weeds dictionary.

compost tea — A popular summer beverage among gardeners.

dust — mud with the juice squeezed out.

earthworms — terrestrial invertebrates with tube-like bodies that improve soil fertility by consuming large pieces of organic matter and converting them into rich humus and that occasionally make you feel grateful that they're doing that job and not you.

fence — a barrier, typically of wood or wire, enclosing an area of ground to mark a boundary, control access, or prevent escape, and an object of endless mockery by rabbits, moles, deer, raccoons, and every other creature that routinely passes over, under, around, or through it.

fertilizer — a substance added to soil to increase its fertility and that you sometimes feel like throwing at people in the hope they will grow up.

gardening — a frilly word for weeding.

garden centers — sites of mass hypnosis, typically resulting in people blissfully turning over a good deal of their money; way stations where plants are briefly stored on their journey from their farms or greenhouses of origin to the homes where they will be brought to die.

green fingers — something everyone else has plenty of, or claims to.

hybrid plants — plants that combine sunlight with an electric motor to power the plant.

knees — devices for finding rocks in one's garden.

perennial — this year maybe, but next year doubtful.

seed catalogs — fictional fables with fantasy photos.

porch — a covered shelter projecting from the front entrance of a house and where, during the summer, wasps build nests beneath and neighbors deposit excess zucchini above.

shovel — a highly efficient back-pain generator, sold as loss leaders by chiropractors, osteopaths, and massage therapists.

sphagnum — a word most gardeners don't even like to think about, let alone say out loud.

sprinkling can — the proper but painfully slow way of applying water to the roots of plants.

weed — a plant that shouldn't be there and has no plans to move.

weeds — generally indigenous, native populations that gardeners seek forcibly to evict from the land.

What it says . . . and what it means

Experienced gardeners can spot the code phrases on seed packages and in gardening catalogs, magazines, and websites and understand what they really mean. Here's your Quippery translation guide:

What it says . . .	**What it really means . . .**
A favorite of birds	Avoid planting near cars, sidewalks, or clotheslines
More beautiful each year	Unsightly
Zone 5 with added protection	Very risky
May require support	Engineering experience advised
Moisture-loving	Plant it in wetlands
Carefree	You'll have no effect on this plant's vitality
Vigorous	Invasive species
Annuals	Disappointing for only one season

Hardy	Survives adverse conditions in anyone else's garden
Tender	Magnet for deer and rabbits and insects

From Henry Beard, *A Gardener's Dictionary*

Henry Beard is the American humorist and author who helped found the magazine *National Lampoon.* In his book *A Gardener's Dictionary*, he offers his own wry take on key gardening terms:

Annual — Any plant that dies before blooming. *See* PERENNIAL.

Autumn — Delightful season that runs from the disposal of the last zucchini to the arrival of the first catalog.

Bulb — Potential flower buried in autumn, never to be seen again.

Eggplant — Purplish, meaty vegetable whose taste when cooked — which depends considerably on the method of preparation, and there are many — has been variously compared to burnt liver, fried sandals, scorched clams, a wallet, old magazines, and mud.

Hoeing — A manual method of severing roots from stems of newly planted flowers and vegetables.

Hose — Crude, but effective and totally safe type of scythe towed through gardens to flatten flower beds and level vegetable plantings.

Perennial — any plant which, had it lived, would have bloomed year after year. *See* ANNUAL.

Seed — Costly, but highly nutritious form of bird food sold in handsome packets printed with colorful pictures of flowers and vegetables.

Zucchini — The only vegetable with its own ZIP code.

Got tricked into going to a basketball game. Turns out there's no garden at Madison Square

REPOTTED

addy
@MVRTINEZ23

Rip to my plant .. I tried man ..you know that😭

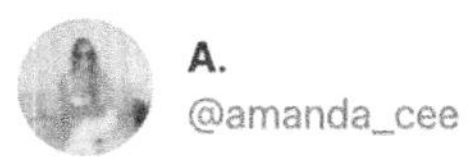

A.
@amanda_cee

RIP to my tomato plant. death by white fly infestation.

Anissa Saada
@AnissaSaada

Some people my age have kids and I'm googling "house plants that are impossible to kill" diversity is beautiful

succulent: WHAT THE FUCK ARE YOU DOING
me: it's been a few weeks, i thought you might want some water
succulent: NO

The houseplant died inside, so I threw it out, and now it's growing in the driveway just to spite me.

therapist: how have you been doing this week

me: i purchased several new succulents

therapist: [scribbles "not good" in her notes]

"I'm not obsessed"

Also me:

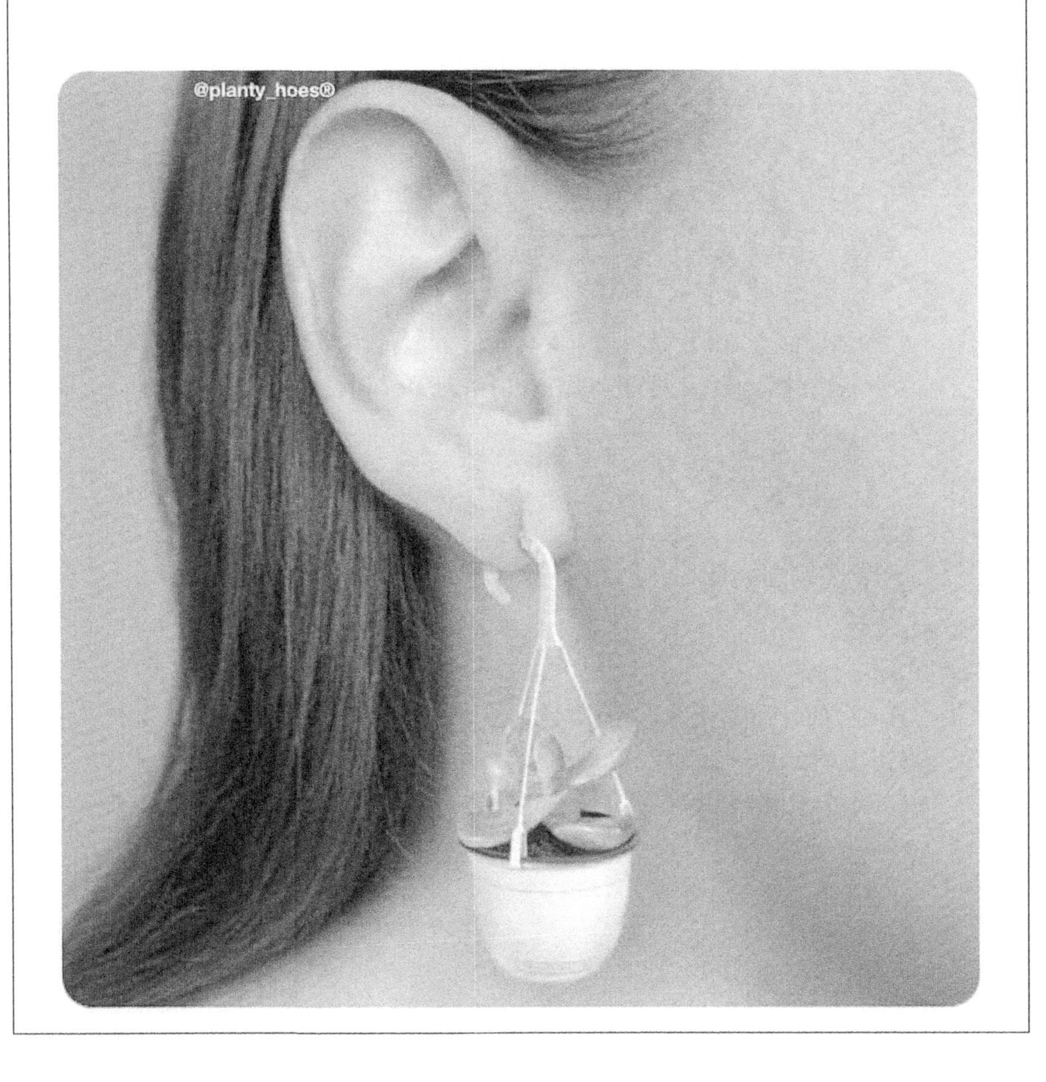

twitter trolls don't faze me bc i was once brutally dragged in a houseplant forum for overwatering my fiddle leaf fig tree and i haven't felt anything since

i think my plant is dying idk what to do i give it water and sunlight please help it doesn't have health insurance

at a bar
BARTENDER: this is from the gentleman over there
GIRL: this is a plant
ME [shouting from across the bar]: just wanted to say aloe

owl lang syne
@tytonidaeus
Went to check why one of my plants was lopsided in its pot and......oh.....

Replying to @CaucasianJames

my plants death is going viral. just how he wanted it to

Jewel Staite
@JewelStaite

Charlie went to put one of our outdoor plants in the garage and I said, "What are you doing?! It'll die!" And he said, "... It's fake. It's a fake plant. Wait. Have you been watering this?"
For three years. It was the only plant I was successfully keeping alive.

Got plants in your pants?

Lerwick, Shetland Islands

GAME OF THORNS

THE DIFFERENCE BETWEEN NON-GARDENERS AND GARDENERS

Objects or events	Non-gardener perception or response	Gardener perception or response
Compost	Vermin, filth, bubonic plague	Powerful potion
Falling leaves	A wasted weekend	Fodder for compost
Rabbit	Peter Rabbit	Peter Raptor
Chipmunk	Alvin, Chip, & Dale	Underground metropolis
Squirrel	Fluffy tail, fun to feed	Contortionist that destroys birdfeeders while twisted into the shape of a pretzel

Objects or events	Non-gardener perception or response	Gardener perception or response
Wild violets in the lawn	"Horrors! Grab the weed killer!"	"Hooray! Grab the camera."
5" tall front yard grass	Shame, stay indoors, pull down the shades	Healthy, green grass at the perfect height
Two cubic yards of clean, composted cow manure	Twenty cubic yards of freshly dropped cow manure	Two cubic yards that guarantee a great garden
Hanging plants	Décor	Hanging cuttings, waiting to be plucked
Car	Status symbol	Something used to haul plants and mulch
Plastic plant	Plant	Oxymoron
Someone planting a rhododendron in full sun	Someone planting a plant	Someone inflicting cruel and unusual punishment
Someone wiring a bonsai	Someone inflicting cruel and unusual punishment	A master artisan helping a plant reach perfection

Objects or events	Non-gardener perception or response	Gardener perception or response
A visit to the desert outside of Las Vegas	“Get me out of here!”	“I never knew the desert could be so beautiful.”
A visit to a Las Vegas casino	“I never knew a town could be so exciting.”	“Get me out of here!”
A visit to Redwood National Park	“I’m wet, cold, and 300 miles from San Francisco.”	“Who wouldn’t thought that heaven was only 300 miles from San Francisco?”
An old-fashioned garden center	“Where are the gas grills?”	“What’s the spending limit on my credit card?”
Plastic bags filled with leaves	Bags of garbage	Free bags of mulch for next year’s garden
People buying canned corn in the summer	People buying corn	People who’ve forgotten to take their medication
People wearing Wellie boots	People who’ve forgotten to take their medication	Potential life-long companions

CAUTION
BEWARE OF GARDENER

CHEESY PEASY

All right, we admit it — the stuff in this section is as corny as it gets. No need to reveal your lowbrow taste — just go ahead and enjoy, groan, laugh, or whatever it is you do.

Pun runs

- Ah, it's summer thyme!
- Lettuce turnip the beet.
- Frog parking only. All others will be toad.
- I love you from my head tomatoes.
- I fought the lawn and the lawn won.
- Weed it and reap.
- Give a weed an inch and it'll take a yard.

Riddle quiddle

Q: What kind of socks does a gardener wear?

A: Garden hose!

Q: Why didn't anyone laugh at the gardener's jokes?

A: Because they were too corny!

Q: Why did the tomato blush?

A: Because he saw the salad dressing!

Q: Which vegetable did Noah leave off the ark?

A: Leeks!

Q: What's the easiest way to stop a dog from digging in the garden?

A: Take away his shovel!

Q: Why can't the flower ride his bike?

A: Because he lost his petals!

Q: What do trees drink?

A: Root beer!

Q: What kind of
flower looks like it just came
back from a
fight?

A: A Black-Eyed Susan!

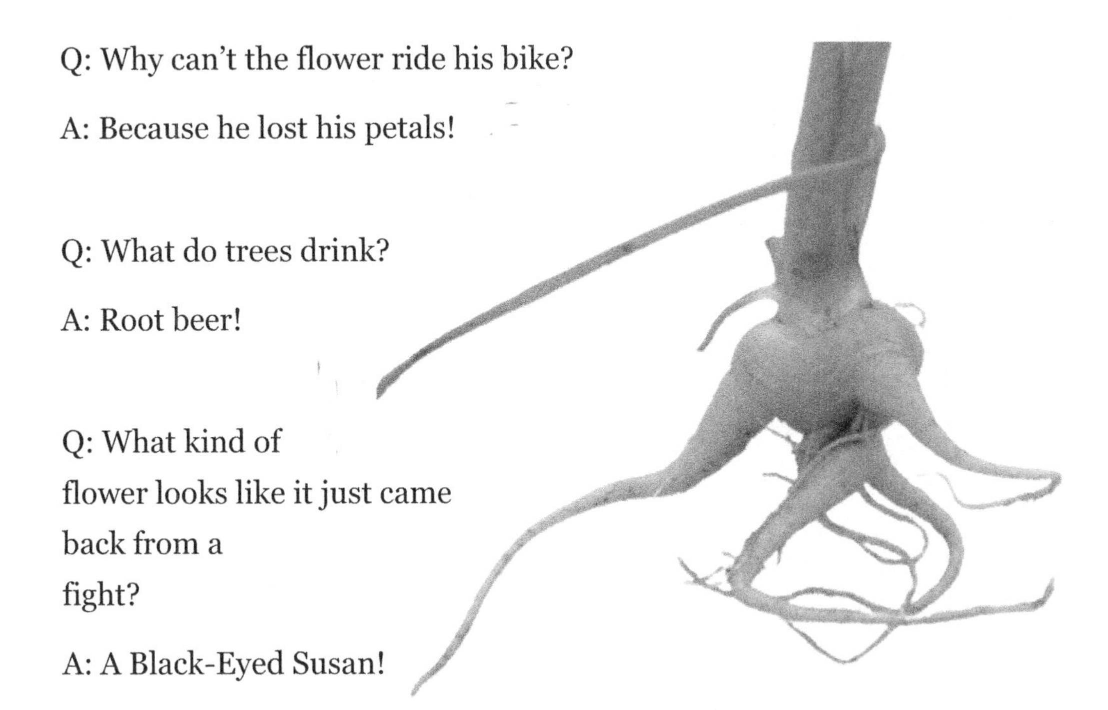

Q: What happened to the plant in math class?

A: It grew square roots!

Q: What do you get if you divide the circumference of a pumpkin by its diameter?

A: Pumpkin pi (π)!

You may think this is a corner of lettuce, but it's really just the tip of the iceberg.

Moaners & groaners

My gardener talked to me about edible herbs I can grow.

It was sage advice.

I stood in my garden early yesterday morning
wondering where the sun had gone.

Then it dawned on me.

So my neighbor sees
me kneeling down, busy
in my garden and asks what I'm doing.

"I'm putting all my plants in alphabetical order."

"Really? I don't know how you find the time!"

"It's right next to the sage"

I started growing some fungi in my garden, but it failed miserably.

I guess there is mushroom for improvement.

My wife is furious at our next-door neighbor who sunbathes nude in her garden.

Personally, I'm on the fence.

I have a birdfeeder in the garden.

It also works as a cat feeder.

Q: How did the millionaire gardener get rich so quick?

A: He was running a huge pansy scheme.

Q: Why is the Incredible Hulk such a good gardener?

A: He's got green fingers.

Q: We've got his and hers bathrooms, his and hers cars, his and hers bank accounts — so what would we have if there were his and hers garden sheds?

A: He shed she shed.

I used to make loads of money clearing leaves from gardens.
I was raking it in.

Yet again, someone has added more soil to my allotment
The plot thickens. . . .

Q: What is the gardener's favorite novel?

A: *War and Peas*

A friend dug a hole in the garden and filled it with water.
I think he meant well.

Q: Why did the gardener quit?

A: His celery wasn't high enough.

Q: What do you get if you cross a four-leaf clover with poison ivy?

A: A rash of good luck.

Q: What do you call it when earthworms take over the world?

A: Global worming.

I used to have a job making furniture out of plants.
I'll tell you, it was no bed of roses.

Q: Why shouldn't you tell a secret in a garden?

A: Because the potatoes have eyes and the corn has ears!

I'm making a belt decorated with herbs from my garden.
My friends tell me it's a waist of thyme.

It turns out my front lawn is chicken proof.
It's impeccable.

Q: What is brown and runs round the garden?

A: A fence.

Q: What do you call a homeless snail?

A: A slug.

Q: Why couldn't the gardener plant any flowers?

A: He hadn't botany!

Q: What do you call a nervous tree?
A: A sweaty palm!

Q: What position does a baby plant serve in the army?

A: Infant tree.

Q: What kind of vegetable do you get when an elephant walks through your garden?

A: Squash.

I want to tell you about a girl
who only eats plants . . .
But you've probably heard of herbivore.

Did you hear about the gardener who went crazy?

He was hearing voices in his shed.

I can cut down a tree just by looking at it.
It's true! I saw it with my own eyes.

Q: Why was the cucumber mad?

A: Because it was in a pickle!

My wife told me I planted the wrong flowers. . . .
Oopsie daisy.

Q: Why did the cabbage win the race?

A: Because it was ahead!

A single ant can live to be 29 years old.
OK — what about a married one?

GARDENERS
We're At The
Weeding Edge
Quippery

BLAINE WAS HAVING SECOND THOUGHTS ABOUT PLANTING THE MARDI GRASS

 offthemark.com

MANGO MENACE

from Dave Barry

"I'm busy worrying about being killed by our mango tree"

I'm busy worrying about being killed by our mango tree. Our new yard has a mango tree, which I bet sounds like exotic fun to those of you who live in normal climates, right? Just think of it! All the mangoes you need, right in your own yard!

The problem is that, mango-wise, you don't need a whole lot. You take one bite, and that takes care of your mango needs until at least the next presidential administration. But the mangoes keep coming. They're a lot like zucchini, which erupt out of the ground far faster than you could eat them even if you liked them, which nobody does, so you start lugging hundreds of pounds of zucchini to your office in steel-reinforced shopping bags, hoping your co-workers will be stupid enough to take some home, except of course they're lugging in *their* zucchini, all summer long, tons of them coming in, until the entire office building collapses in a twisted tangle of girders and telephone message slips and zucchini pulp, out of which new vines start to spring immediately.

Mangoes are even worse, because a) they grow on trees, and b) they're about the size of a ladies' bowling ball, only denser. They're the kind of fruit that would be designed by the Defense Department. They hang way up in our tree, monitoring the yard and communicating with each other via photosynthesis, and whenever they see me approaching, they fire off a Warning Mango, sending one of their number thundering to Earth, cratering our lawn and alarming seismologists as far away as Texas ("The Silly Hat State"). Even on the ground, the mango remains deadly, because it immediately rots and becomes infested with evil little flies, and if you try to kick it off the lawn, it explodes, a mango grenade, covering your body with a repulsive substance known to botanists as "mango poop" that stays on your sneakers forever, so that when you go out in public, your feet are obscured by a cloud of flies, and the Florida natives snicker and say to each other, "Look! That idiot kicked a mango!"

— *Dave Barry Talks Back*

QUESTiONS & ANTHERS

Every gardener, matter how experienced, runs into situations where they're uncertain what to do. Our Quippery gardening experts are here to help.

My raspberries yield almost no berries — it's like they don't know what they're supposed to do.

Don't forget that raspberries need to be trained, just like any other pet. When they *do* produce a nice berry, reward them with a couple of fertilizer pellets. In 3–4 weeks you should see better results.

My entire garden has just been wiped out by a 100-year mid-summer hailstorm.

Allow yourself to grieve, but not too long. Embrace the new reality: You now have a super low-maintenance garden. Enjoy, friend.

My garden has been invaded by moles — they're starting to turn my garden into Swiss cheese.

You need to build a wall around your garden. You'll want to go 6-7 feet deep.

That's going to be expensive.

You get the moles to pay for it.

I can't grow blueberries in my garden no matter what. I've spent seven years at it, adjusting soil pH, adding compost, sulfur, other soil amendments, mulch combinations. Nada!

Go to the supermarket and buy yourself some nice packages of organic blueberries. Save your money and enjoy. Take it easy, friend.

My plants only want to listen to classical music — in fact they thrive on it — but I prefer rock 'n' roll.

Try some Emerson, Lake, and Palmer and see how they feel. If that resonates, experiment with some other prog rock outfits. Otherwise — cue up the three B's and enjoy.

Can I have sex in my garden if no one can see?

Sure!

We planted an apple tree sapling in our yard and loved it so much we decided to plant a second sapling. We never expected they would be bickering constantly.

This not uncommon problem is known as *sapling rivalry*. There are some simple solutions. Each day, spend a few minutes with each sapling individually. Every week or two, spend more "alone time" with each sapling, engaging in an activity together that you both enjoy. And be sure to do things with both together.

My garden has become so politically divided that the plants are hardly communicating — some refuse even to pollinate.

We hear a lot of this.

First: Establish some boundaries. Boundary number one: No talking about politics.

Keep the focus on the things the plants enjoy in common: sun, soil, and rain. And, of course, pollinating.

How do you make compost tea?

The recipe is simple:

1. Scoop a quarter-cup of compost from your compost pile.

2. Drop into a large pitcher, fill with boiling water, and steep 5 minutes.
3. Add a sprig of fresh peppermint or spearmint (preferably from your garden) and a dash of lemon juice.
4. Serve hot or cold. Enjoy.

What have you heard about breakfast compost compote?

AH! Now there's a thing! Just when people were wondering how to take the blah out of breakfast, along comes breakfast compost compote, and it's taking the breakfast world by storm.

Compotes and compost have both been around for ages, and it's amazing that it's only now that people have made the connection. The words are so similar they practically beg to be turned into each other.

If you want to make an epic pancake or waffle brunch, top them with sweet compost compote — and making it is as easy as pie.

In a saucepan, combine 4 cups of compost, 1 cup of water, and ½ cup of organic sugar. If you're feeling crazy, add a tablespoon of brandy. Over medium heat, bring the mixture to a boil, thickening to your desired consistency, maybe 2-3 minutes.

Besides pancakes or waffles, you can also use it to top French toast, oatmeal, yogurt, ice cream, and popcorn.

In the unlikely event you have anything left over that no one can eat, you know what to do — compost it.

One of my plants is shedding its outer layer.

That plant is a snake. It knows what it's doing. Let it do its thing.

Sometimes I get so frustrated with my garden that I lose it and unload my stress on them. So much work, such low yields. What should I do?

Your plants are very sensitive — you don't want to damage their self-esteem. So DON'T criticize them directly (e.g., "You guys are totally worthless"). But DO let them know how their behavior makes YOU feel: "When you guys stiff me like this, it makes me feel like a failure . . . and like you're totally worthless."

Woe betide me! Woe, woe, and thrice woe. The word —

No —

Yes! The word —

No! Please don't say —

The word *sphagnum* has —

Please stop! We implore —

— *sphagnum* has taken me hostage. How dark, how baleful that word! And now pronouncing —

Please stop — please —

— pronouncing itself over and over in my mind — the ancient, malevolent curse — *sphagnum sphagnum sphagnum sphagnum* — like the tolling, tolling, tolling of a bell. Someone, anyone — I'm begging you, please rescue me.

Very well, then! We recoil from even having to think about this — but you leave us no option. Your affliction is rare but very real and very serious. It can also be contagious, so take care to isolate until you're thoroughly rid of it. Here's the medically recommended procedure:

- *Do not try to push it out* — you'll *sphagnum* only be feeding it your energy. And your energy is exactly *sphagnum* what it craves.
- Now you will try gradually to wean yourself of the word. Start *sphagnum* by replacing it with similar-sounding words and then move to less similar words.
- Most people start with *sphagnous* (meaning *of, relating to, or abounding in sphagnum*).
- From *sphagnous* you move to *sphygmus* (a pulse or pulsation) and then to *sphygmic* (relating to the pulse).

- And from there you move further away, to words like *sphincter* and *sputum*, increasing your distance step *sphagnum* by step.

In this way, if you're patient and persistent, you may be able ease yourself free. Your best bet, though, is probably *sphagnum* an exorcist.

WASCALLY WABBITS:
GOING TO BATTLE FOR YOUR BLOOMS

by Meredith Siemsen

If you know me at all, you know I'm a sucker when it comes to animals, especially small furry ones. In the fall, my mother gets angry with me when I swerve the car to avoid running over fuzzy wuzzy caterpillars on the highway. "Why would you risk my life for a caterpillar!?" I can totally see her point, but it's almost involuntary. There are very few of God's creatures that I feel comfortable extinguishing: basically just ticks, mosquitos, bagworms, brown marmorated stink bugs — you know, invasive species and disease-spreading pests. I can justify those.

But in the past few years, I've developed an almost murderous disdain for a certain cute-as-a-button, spawned-from-Satan critter. This loathsome and vicious beast has caused me sleepless nights and fits of rage, not to mention dollar after hard-earned dollar. He is the vilest of the lagomorphs, the most loathsome of the low-bellied lapins. It's not popular to hold this kind of grudge during the month of Easter — sorry, kids — but Mr. Peter Cottontail . . . you can go shove it.

I never had an issue with rabbits until I started getting serious about gardening. My fever for growing pretty things began with a patio-potted hibiscus and some colorful coleus one summer and blossomed from there. I got hooked. I started helping friends and family members with their gardens, and before I knew it I was designing flowerbeds for a handful of clients around town.

A few years back I got a job reestablishing perennial flowers around a large domicile on Fairfield's north side. The owner of the home remarked that previous gardeners had planted several things, but much of it had petered out. That's weird, I thought — perennials are meant to come back year after year. Maybe they suffered a couple hard winters or weren't suited to the soil type or light conditions? And there is a semi-deplorable trend for flower sellers to label certain plants as perennials when in all likelihood, in Iowa, they will behave like annuals (dead as a doornail come winter). I've had many a success with plants bought from all kinds of greenhouses, but buyer beware. Do your research first if you're looking for a perennial that acts like a perennial.

Anyway, I was up for the challenge of this new job, excited to bring some color back to the property, but it wasn't until after I started putting a few things in the ground that I realized what part of the issue might have been. The place was a haven for rabbits. Hungry ones.

Day after demoralizing day I would walk onto the property and see new damage that those blasted cottontails had done to my fresh plantings. That first summer in particular, anyone within earshot would have heard me weaving a tapestry of obscenities as I walked from bed to bed. "Hellfire and damnation!! Those scumbags! Those a-holes!" I have a potty mouth when I see a perfectly good bloom just lying there decapitated on the ground with that telltale diagonal bite mark on its stem. Sufferin' succotash!

There are certain flowers that those blasted bunnies will just eat like salad — blooms, leaves, stem, everything. Thinking about putting petunias in your yard? Nasturtiums? Tulips? Think again.

With the uncanny number of wabbits around this particular neighborhood — procreating regularly every four to six weeks—the sight of a baby bunny was no longer cute. In fact, babies are the worst culprits. Younger rabbits haven't learned yet which plants they don't like, so they'll bite into anything that seems remotely like food, just to have a taste. Once they've taken a chomp, they might not even want a second mouthful — but I've seen them happily leveling off a stand of lilies while they experiment with their palates. Jerks.

The most heartbreaking moment of that first year was when I bought some lavender plants in full bloom and, as an experiment, left them unplanted in the lawn for a good week to observe any possible nibbling. Every time I checked, they looked fine. No snacking. Dare I?

I finally decided it was safe to put them in the ground. The next morning — you guessed it — I came back to check on them and they'd been mowed down by some rabid little rabbit mouths! Those little wieners!! It's like they were just messing with me!!!

This past season, however, I got a sweet little taste of justice. I'd heard reports of a stray black cat skulking around the neighborhood, and I began discovering intermittent evidence of its hunts. I did not mind finding rabbit carcasses behind various hedges. I secretly celebrated. I'm just glad I got there after the nefarious deed was done. . . .

Amy Flory
@FunnyIsFamily

I used to root for Peter Rabbit, but now that I have a garden of my own I'm team Mr. McGregor all the way.

WORLD NAKED GARDENING DAY

Yes, this is a thing. It started in 2005 and quickly spread around the world, celebrated by gardeners and nongardeners. In the US it's the first Saturday in May each year.

Laura, author of the gardening blog over at youshouldgrow.com, helpfully gives us a list of things you shouldn't do on this day:

- Plant roses
- Re-pot your cacti
- Go to the community garden
- Fire up the hedge trimmer
- Forget to bring props
- Forget to put on sunblock
- Pose in a wheelbarrow
- Squat in the bushes
- Climb a tree
- Forget a way to carry your cell phone

- Don't do it alone

Laura adds some things you *should* do: Have fun with it, include your whole family, invite your friends, and stay in your comfort zone.

GARDENING IN THE HEADLINES

...at will Fit

The Daily News

chan...

...l. LXIX. . .No. 54 NEW NEWS FOR TODAY! The News.com *Price:* $...

Child's Stool Great For Use in Garden

Findings verified at international symposium.

...ffalo, Nov. 2. Researchers at an ...national symposium in Fair... ...unced an exciting

...ace Talks

Local news:

Stolen Pumpkins Found by Tree

MINNEOLA, Ks (AP) —

Turns out it was another case of "hiding in plain sight," according to Minneola Police Chief Ruth Lesse. In a case that had stumped local authorities for weeks, seven pumpkins that were stolen on November 2

The Daily Post

Vol. LXIX. . .No. 54 NEW NEWS FOR TODAY! The News.com *Price: $5.00*

Cold Wave Linked to Temperatures

Confirmed by NOAA

By Idy Claire, Daily Post Staff Reporter

Washington, DC, Nov. 2 – Data compiled by the National Oceanic and Atmospheric Admininstration over the past two years has led researchers to speculate that the recent cold wave is actually the result of temperature. In a

Regional news:

Farmer Bill Dies in House

By Fay Slift, Daily Post Reporter

Washington, DC – Despite massive bipartisan public support, a bill that would give American farmers substantial annual payments for not growing eggplant, rutabagas, and turnips has failed to make it out of the US House of Representatives. The powerful eggplant, rutabaga, and turnip lobbies, noted for their large campaign contributions to candidates of both parties, had little

imes

Todays weather

If the rain doesn't stop soon it will last for a while.

The News.com *Price: $1.00*

ton State

Regional news:

of Board

Crime stoppers news:

Thieves Steal Corn; Charged With Stalking

HILLSVILLE, Va (AP) —

Hillsville Police Commissioner Amanda B. Reckonwithe announced Thursday that, in conjunction with the FBI, NSA, CIA and

THE GREAT KALE INHALE

Hot dogs, hamburgers, eggs, sausages — there have long been the staples in food eating contests.

Fortunately, now there are more contests that gardeners can contribute to.

Take the Taste of Buffalo Food Festival in 2016, in Buffalo, New York, where the food eating events included the world's first kale eating contest.

The event drew elite competitive eaters from around the country. And the winner would be the person who ingested the most kale in eight minutes.

"It's the new frontier food in major league eating," declared Crazy Legs Conti, one of America's winningest eaters and the title holder for wolfing down the most corn on the cob and French green beans in single sittings. Conti is 45 but boasts of having "the stomach of a 19-year-old."

But Conti was trounced by Georgia's Gideon "The Truth" Oji. Oji, a native of Nigeria, polished off 25 ½ bowls of kale — more than half of the kale consumed by all nine competitors put together.

That's more than three bowls of kale a minute, or more than one bowl every 20 seconds. By comparison, most mere mortals require five or six minutes to eat a single forkful of kale, and some never get even that far.

Kale and hearty

Festival attendees absolutely loved watching the competition.

"It was disgusting," said Mike Polino, attending with his wife and teenage daughter and initially drawn to the event out of curiosity.

How about the competitors, elite eaters one and all?

"It got a little stuck in your throat and went up in your nasal passages," said Michael Dietz, who has eaten more pumpkin pie and fried mushrooms in single sittings than anyone alive.

"Just trying to stuff it so fast and not then to get your mouth stuffed, got pretty hard," said Eric "Badlands" Booker, who lifted the bowl above his head, the better to dump kale into his mouth. Although Booker only placed fourth, he did emerge triumphant in the unofficial contest for who could slosh the greatest amount of liquid and kale down one's front.

And the winner, Gideon Oji? "I'm still hungry," he said, after downing more than 25 bowls of kale and walking away with $2,000 and the highly coveted gleaming green metal "Kale Cup" loaded with kale. "I'm going to go eat some real food."

— Based on an actual news story. The characters' names and statements and the name and location of the festival have not been changed.

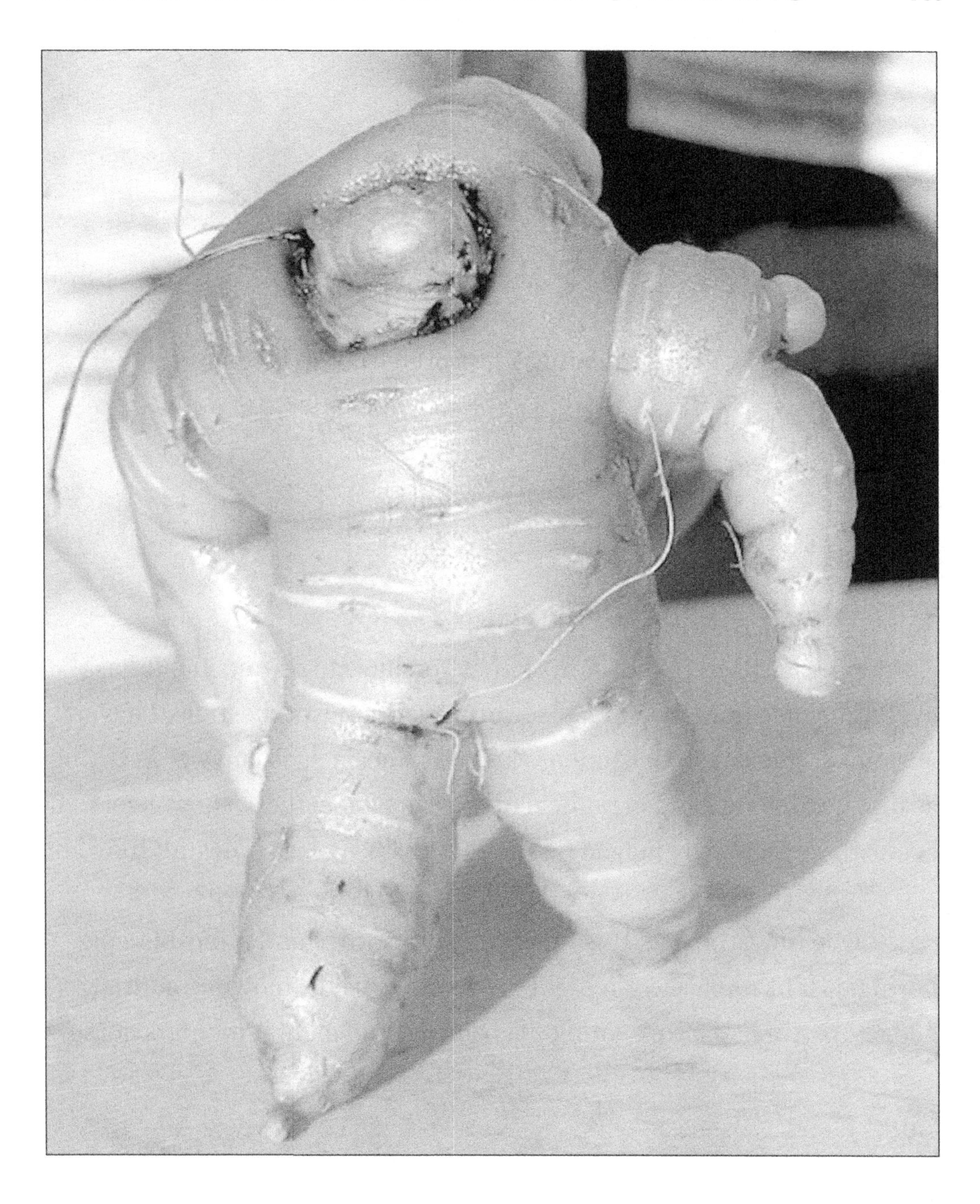

MAD HATERS

I have nothing against gardening. I just prefer not to be there when it happens.

— Tracy Macleod

Why I hate gardening

Gardening is talked-up housework that you have to do outside. It has everything in common with housework, even some of the tools. I have a vacuum cleaner that I use indoors and out since it sucks up wet as happily as dry. Gardening has a great deal of the same objective as housework and is mostly depressingly judged on the same criteria — is it neatandtidy and is it weed-free, alongside is it neatandtidy and is it dust-free?

Gardening is boring. It is repetitious, repetitive and mind-blowing boring, just like housework. All of it — sowing seeds, mowing, cutting hedges, potting up, propagating — is boring, and all of it requires doing over and over again. If there are enjoyable jobs they're mostly enjoyable for the result not the process.

There is no actual intellectual content to the task itself, even if there may be in the planning and designing.

— Anne Wareham, *The Bad-Tempered Gardener*

The best thing about gardening is that if you put it off long enough, it won't be necessary.

— Unknown

A garden is like those pernicious machineries we read of, every month, in the newspapers, which catch a man's coat-skirt or his hand, and draw in his arm, his leg, and his whole body to irresistible destruction.

— Ralph Waldo Emerson

Replying to @bridger_w

have u ever been a plant before? stuck in that spot your whole life? Id take what I can get too

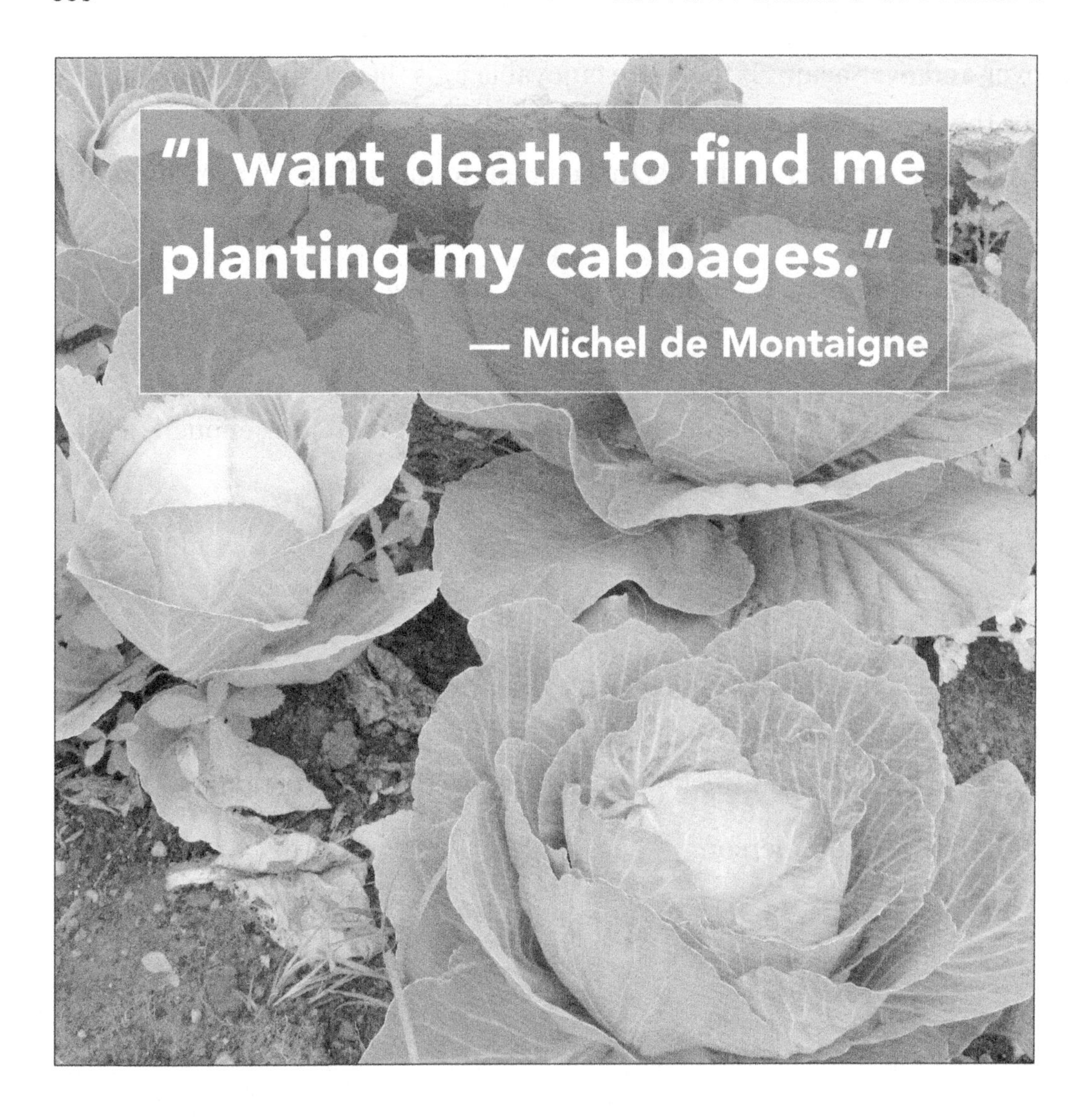
"I want death to find me planting my cabbages."
— Michel de Montaigne

CARROTS iN LOVE

Of all the things that grow in gardens, are there any plants that "get it on" more explicitly than carrots?

At least they have the discretion to do their thing underground — giving new meaning to the expression *doing the dirty*.

Except that when you pull them up, they don't cease and desist — they just keep on choogling, oblivious to all onlookers.

Onlookers, meanwhile, are either staring in rapt fascination or trying without success to avert their eyes.

If you've ever wondered where baby carrots come from, now you know.

In this section: a collection of cute, cozying, cuddling, coupling *carrots.*

Cue up Lionel Richie, "All Night Long."

Parental discretion advised.

Fave song:
"Hold On," Michael Bublé

Fave song:
"Wrapped Up In You,"
Garth Brooks

Fave song:
"In My Arms,"
Kylie Minogue

Fave song:
"Soul to
Squeeze,"
Red Hot Chili
Peppers

What the hell are they spraying on vegetables these days?

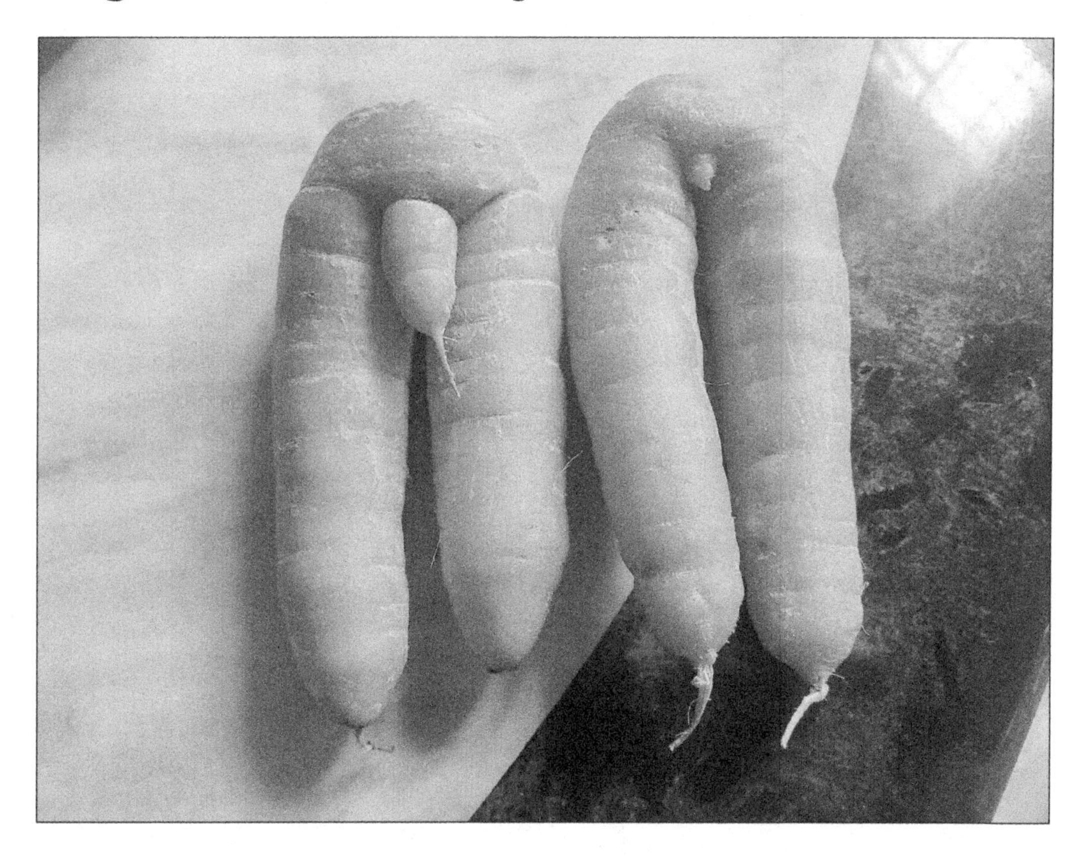

This photo, posted on Reddit with the caption above, inspired some funny comments:

"You vs. the guy she told you not to worry about."

"Me in DMs vs. me in real life."

"Same thing they are using to turn the frogs gay."

"I want some of whatever they sprayed on the left one."

"Got sprayed with liquid Viagra."

"Those are genitalia modified crops, no doubt about it."

"Puts 'check out the carrots' in that T-Pain song into perspective."

"Looks like the right one was grown with my family genes."

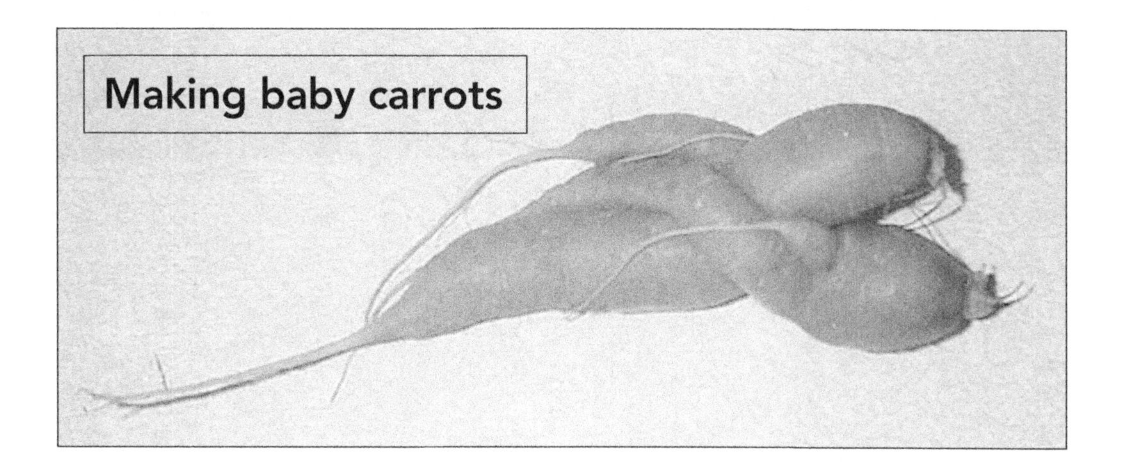

ménage à trois?

HARDY
MUMS
ATLANTIC FEATURE © 1995 MARK PARISI
offthemark.com
MARK PARISI

Putting seeds and plants in the soil, doing some weeding and watering, then harvesting baskets of veggies and bouquets of flowers — is that all there is to it? Think again.

People who think they can run the earth should begin with a small garden.

— Unknown

To live off a garden, you practically have to live in it.

— Frank McKinney Hubbard

Early to bed, early to rise, work like hell, fertilize.

— Emily Whaley

One of the worst mistakes you can make as a gardener is to think you're in charge.

— Janet Gillespie

An optimistic gardener is one who believes that whatever goes down must come up.

— Lesley Hall

Nothing discourages an amateur gardener like watching his family eat the entire garden at one meal.

— Unknown

Gardening requires lots of water — most of it in the form of perspiration.

— Unknown

Grump's Law of Bulb Survival states that the more you pay for a particularly beautiful bulb, the more slugs and snails will seek it out and destroy it.

— Ivor Grump, *The Grumpy Gardener's Handbook*

Nothing ever looks like it does on the seed packet.

— Unknown

from The Onion

NEWS IN BRIEF

Full Summer of Tending Backyard Garden Produces Single Edible Cherry Tomato

CATOOSA, OK — After months of watering, mulching, staking, fertilizing, pruning, and spraying each plant, local homeowner Margie Helmholtz confirmed Wednesday that an entire summer of tending her backyard garden had yielded one edible cherry tomato. According to sources, Helmholtz paid more than $280 for soil, fencing, pesticides, and specialty gloves and hand tools, and also devoted scores of hours to the study of home gardening, purchasing two books and visiting nearly a dozen websites on the subject prior to reaping her single-tomato harvest. The 39-year-old woman is said to have spent part of each weekend on her hands and knees in the searing heat in order to transplant seedlings to her garden, keep them weeded, and ensure the plants' thorny vines were wrapped correctly around their trellises — actions that, taken together from late May through August, produced exactly one limp tomato approximately one inch in diameter. At press time, sources reported that the cherry tomato tasted fucking awful.

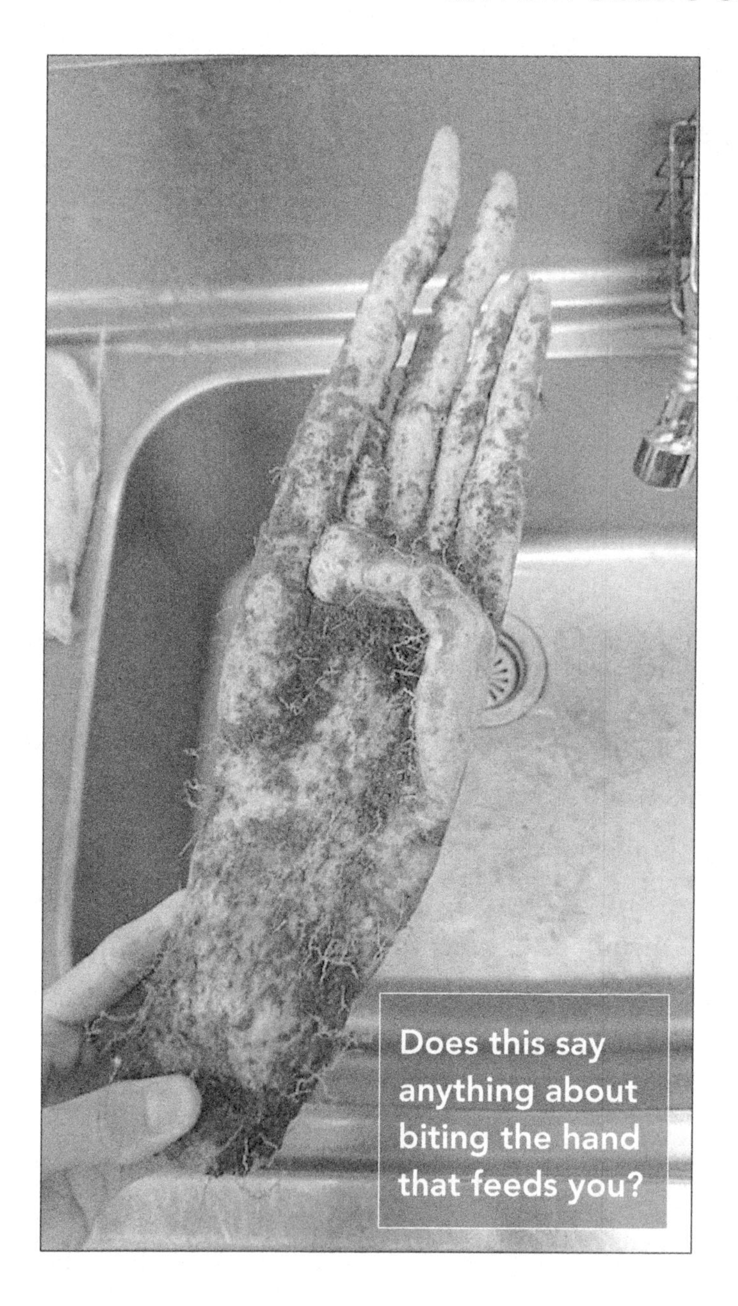
Does this say
anything about
biting the hand
that feeds you?

"When I put a plant or seed in the ground, I feel like I've done a good thing for it and it should respond in kind."
— Janice Wells, *The Gin and Tonic Gardener*

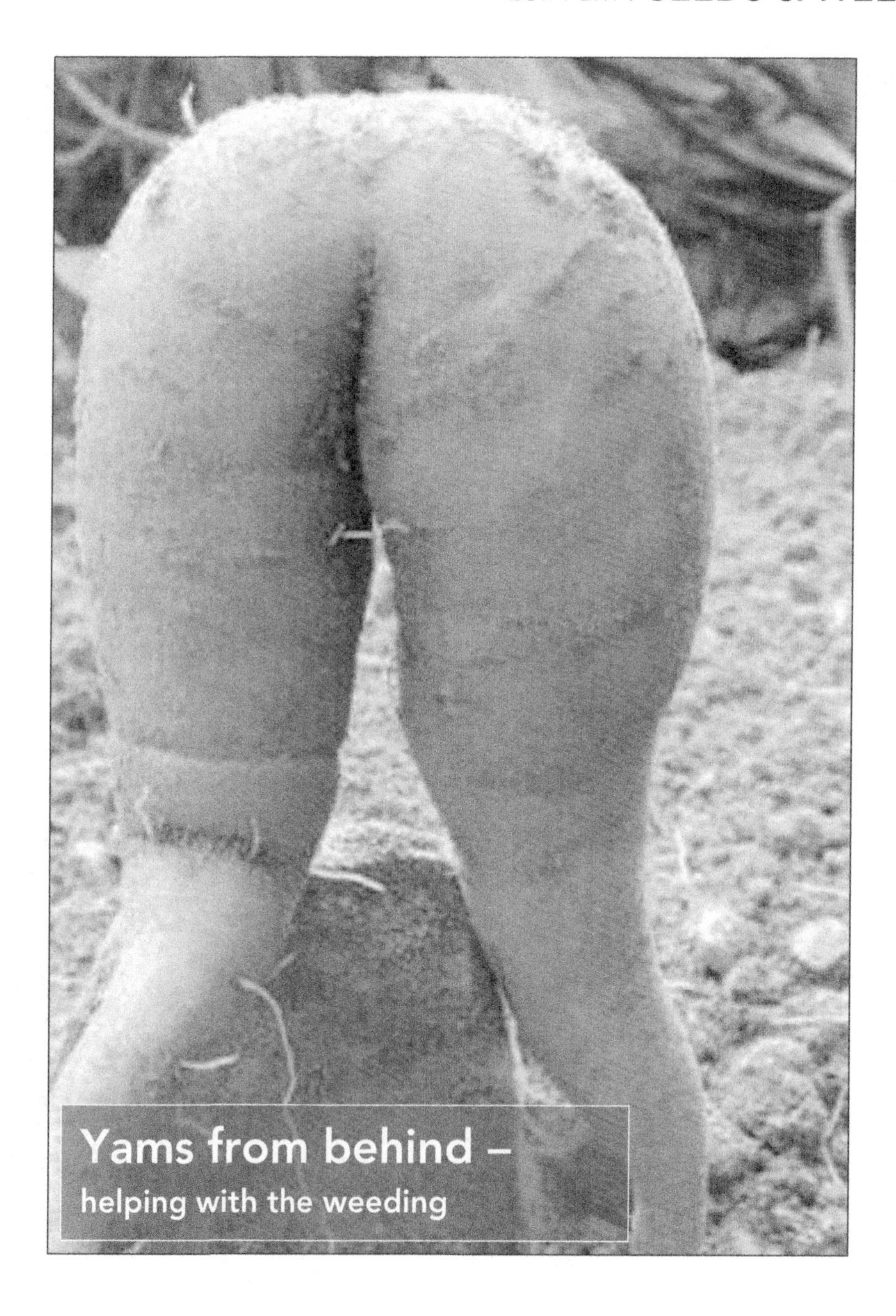

Yams from behind –
helping with the weeding

RETURN ON INVESTMENT

The first tweet prompted a comically cautionary series of replies:

Bizarre Lazar
@BizarreLazar

After 6 weeks, $140 in supplies, and daily watering, we're only three to four weeks away from enjoying a single 25¢ vegetable from our garden.

Mecclesiastes
@Zetetes_MS

Replying to @BizarreLazar

And even then, any one of a score of insect species, funguses, or animals like raccoons, birds & squirrels might very well beat you to that vegetable! Hell, even the neighborhood kids might consider it fun to raid.

Replying to @Zetetes_MS and @BizarreLazar

Do kids still raid gardens?

Replying to @mcneillb @Zetetes_MS and @BizarreLazar

You know kids and their legendary love of vegetables.

Replying to @BizarreLazar

Couple of years ago, $235 of supplies and one tomato. My wife's friends are still laughing at me.

Suzanne Simpson
@llsuzll

Replying to @BizarreLazar

Makes you think though about why it's only twenty-five cents in the store when so much work goes into growing it and so many people are involved in getting it to you...

Mr. MEEKO
@MrMEEKO1

Replying to @BizarreLazar

I just spent 150 on full grown blueberry bushes, realized my soil was bad and that I might need to cut a tree down for to get them enough sun to grow. None of this makes sense.

Mr. Anthropy
@Zwolf666

Replying to @BizarreLazar

After over a month of watering, etc. I actually got one whole strawberry yesterday. Granted, it was a really good strawberry...

chuy baca
@chuybaca

Replying to @BizarreLazar

I'm really feeling your pain. We've got a ton of $ in our little garden. I know this all to well. I would have done better buying cryptocurrencies and ordering all organic vegetables delivered to my door. Probably still have a couple of dollars in my pocket.

Bobby Blish
@BobbyBlish

After 6 weeks, $140 in supplies in feed, heatlamp, cage, wood chips for a bed, weekly cage cleanings, daily waterings / feeding, etc, plus $200 more for a bigger chicken coop supplies... We're just three to four weeks away from enjoying the most expensive free eggs ever.

GARDENERS
Weeding By Example
Quippery

SPECIAL BONUS FEATURE

OUR QUEST FOR THE FUNNIEST THINGS PEOPLE HAVE SAID

FOOTPRINTS

"If you come to Africa, stop by and see us in Tanzania."

We'd crisscrossed a good deal of the world in our quest for the funniest things people have said — but we hadn't been to Africa. This pithy email piqued our curiosity.

We were in Uzbekistan at the time. To our surprise, there was a direct flight between Tashkent and Dar es Salaam, the two capital cities. We booked seats for the next day.

The flight was 17 hours. Arriving in Dar es Salaam — on the Indian Ocean, just across from Zanzibar — we learned it would take almost that many hours to drive to our destination.

That drive took us north and west, past Mount Kilimanjaro National Park to a little village called Engare Sero.

But long before we reached Engare Sero, we could see *Ol Doinyo Lengai – Mountain of God* – the 7,600-foot active volcano that looms above the village.

Northern Tanzania is home to the Massai tribe, known worldwide for their bright red dress, their music and singing and dancing, and their intricate jewelry.

But it was not the Massai who had invited us. It was a group of researchers from Appalachian State University.

We were greeted by Cindy Denisova, the leader of the team.

"Gentlemen, welcome to Engare Sero," she said. "Glad you could take us up on our invitation."

Without further formalities, she drove us out to the site she and her team had been investigating.

"This, my friends," she said, waving her arm across the stretch of darkish gray mudflat in front of us, "is one of the most spectacular discoveries of human footprints ever found."

"What makes it so special?" one of us asked.

"Two things," she said. "First, this site has more footprints than any other site discovered so far — more than four hundred all together in this one spot. Second, they're extraordinarily well preserved."

"How old are they?"

"We've dated them between 5,000 and 19,000 years old," she said.

"So they were modern humans."

"Yes," Denisova said. "Anatomically modern humans, just like us."

"And the oldest footprints ever found? Where are they, and how old?"

"There are a couple of sites along the coast of South Africa with footprints around 120,000 years old," Denisova said. "And some of the oldest prints are not even in Africa. In Great Britain, on a beach in Norfolk, they've found human footprints estimated to be between 850,000 and 950,000 years old, if you can imagine. Then there's a site just about 60 miles southwest of here with footprints that are *3.6 million* years old."

"Not modern humans."

"No — we think they were made by Australopithecus afarensis."

"Family to the famous Lucy," one of us said. "Among our human ancestors."

"Correct."

This site was small, a little larger than a tennis court. But as we looked at it, we began to feel a kinship with these people. We'd seen tools made by ancient people, which was moving. So is seeing the bones and skulls they left behind.

But seeing these people's footprints made them alive to us. As if they had walked through here just a few days ago.

"We felt the same thing when we first arrived," Denisova said, sensing our thoughts. "We still do. We can tell a great deal about what everyday life was like for people just by looking at their footprints."

"Example?"

"We've learned a lot about how ancient people dealt with their children," she said. "The kids pretty much went along and did what their parents did. If the parents were cutting up an animal they'd hunted down, we see from the footprints that the kids were right with them."

"Helicopter kids," one of us quipped.

"Exactly!" Denisova said, laughing.

"It gets even more detailed than that," she said. "A really good tracker can tell you the speed a person was walking, whether they were carrying something, whether they were injured, even what direction they were looking. The super elite trackers seem to have a sixth sense — they can practically tell you what the person was thinking."

"You brought in some people like that?" one of us asked.

She nodded.

"Now," she said, "I want to show you the footprints we thought you especially would find interesting."

She walked us around to the opposite side of the area.

"Take a look," she said, gesturing. "You can see that these people were standing around in a group."

"It looks like about half a dozen people," one of us said.

She nodded again. "And they're men."

"Now take a look at this pair," she said, pointing to a particular set.

We examined them carefully.

"Our expert tracker says this man was bending over at the waist."

"OK. . . ."

"You've heard the expression, *doubled over laughing?"*

"You're kidding."

"The same with this one," she said, motioning to another pair of prints.

"Now look at this man's footprints," she said, before we could say anything more.

We went in close to see if we could detect anything.

"Our tracker tells us he had twisted slightly to his right and was turning back forward, possibly with his right arm outstretched."

"You mean to suggest he was —"

"Yes."

"— clapping the guy next to him on the shoulder?"

"Yes — so it seems."

"So this was a bunch of guys, maybe 17,000 years ago, standing around and —"

"Yes."

"Telling *jokes*?"

She laughed out loud. "That's our best guess," she said.

"Oh, my God."

"Of course, we know nothing about the language they spoke —"

"But they were telling jokes!" one of us said. "Who cares what language? Humor is a universal language."

"That's why we invited you here," Denisova said. "We thought that you guys, of anyone, would appreciate this."

This cemented the bond we were feeling. These guys, living lives we could scarcely comprehend, were standing beneath this very volcano in this very spot, goofing around with each other and telling jokes.

"I'd love to know what they were joking about," one of us said.

"They say humor doesn't translate well from one language or culture to another," the other said. "But if we had something like that tracker's sixth sense, I wonder if we could somehow tune in to that time, to those guys, in this place. I'd like to think we'd be laughing with them."

"In geologic time, they were here, like, just a few moments ago. Like we should still be able to hear the echoes of their voices."

That night we lay out under the stars, *Ol Doinyo Lengai* silhouetted against the dark sky. We reflected on the human story arc, unspooling over millions of years, humanity diffusing around the world yet ultimately one family.

"Tomorrow we drive down to Laetoli," one of us said.

"My thought exactly — to those 3.6-million-year-old footprints."

"Maybe they laughed with each other too."

"Of course — why not?"

The African sun rose the next day and we headed southwest, laying down footprints of our own.

Check out our other Quippery books for more adventure stories from our global quest for the funniest things people have said.

ACKNOWLEDGEMENTS

Great thanks to the people who contributed content to this book.

Cartoons copyrighted by Mark Parisi, permission granted for usage. www.offthemark.com

“Deflowered: A Gardener’s Fall Fantasy of Sex & Death” and “Wascally Wabbits: Going to Battle for Your Blooms,” both by Meredith Siemsen, reprinted with permission from *The Iowa Source*. To read the rest of “Wascally Wabbits,” including useful tips for controlling rabbits, go to iowasource.com/2017/04/07/home2017_04_rabbits/. Thank you, Meredith.

“Gardening With Your Kids” and “Phallic Fungus: Getting Stinkhorn Out of Your Stinkin’ Garden,” both by Kate Whinehall, reprinted with permission from Kate Whinehall. For more great gardening posts by Kate, go to https://katewhinehall.wordpress.com.

“The Garden Madness Test,” by Susan M. Watkins, from her book *Garden Madness: The Unpruned Truth About a Blooming Passion,* reprinted with permission from Sean M. Watkins. Thank you also to David Shipman.

“Zucchini to Feed the Masses,” by Bud Herron, first published in HSJ Online, August 31, 2015, with gratitude to Bud Herron.

"A Scientific Explanation of Why It's Not Our Fault That the Neighborhood Squirrels Started Eating Coffee Beans," by Prisca Bejjani, reprinted with permission from Prisca Bejjani.

"The Plant Passion Test," originally titled "The Mad Gardener Society," reprinted with permission from David Hobson. home.golden.net/~dhobson/madsoc.htm.

"An Olympic Gold for Gardening" reprinted with permission from David Hobson. This material is from his book *Diary of a Mad Gardener: To Boldly Grow Where No One Has Grown Before*, in the chapter entitled "The Grueling Garden." Visit "David Hobson's Green Trips" at gardengripe.blogspot.com.

Material by Henry Beard and Roy McKie from *Gardening: A Gardener's Dictionary* (Workman Publishing, 1982).

Some material in "You've Been Gardening Too Long When . . ." was adapted from David Hobson's Garden Humour website, where visitors contributed items: home.golden.net/~dhobson/contoolong.htm

Material from Ivor Grump, *The Grumpy Gardener's Handbook*, reprinted with permission from Pavilion Books.

"I'm busy worrying about being killed by our mango tree," by Dave Barry, from *Dave Barry Talks Back* (1992), reprinted with permission from Penguin Random House.

"The Great Kale Inhale," adapted from Amber Jamieson, "Kale: 'The disgusting new frontier of major league eating," *The Guardian*, July 10, 2016.

Big props to the genius humorists in the Twittersphere.

Huge shout-out to Unknown for their contributions.

If we haven't properly attributed any content in this book, please notify us and we'll correct it — info@quippery.com.

Photo acknowledgements

Big thanks to everyone whose photos appear in this book. There are three categories of photos: photos in the public domain, which need no attribution; photos for which we received the photographers' permission; and photos (marked CC in the list below) posted under the Creative Commons "Attribution 2.0 Generic (CC BY 2.0)" license –creativecommons.org/licenses/by/2.0/. (Some were posted under the "Attribution-ShareAlike 2.0 Generic (CC BY-SA 2.0)" license – creativecommons.org/licenses/by-sa/2.0/). Both CC licenses require users to specify the photo source and any modifications made to it.

We wish we could have done these in color!

Front cover (CC) – "Lyra's Garden Hands," by Devynia (Flickr) – background removed, colors adjusted.

Page 2 – "Flowers," by George Tan (Flicker – public domain) – cropped, grayscaled.

Page 3 – "Masse florale," by Angelo Brathot (Flickr) – cropped, grayscaled, reduced opacity.

Page 4 (CC) – "Cherry tomatoes," by Edgar Pierce (Flickr) – cropped, grayscaled, reduced opacity.

Page 5 (CC) – "SW bed leafy greens, tomatoes, carrots, broccoli, strawberries," by Jennifer Feuchter (Flickr) – cropped, grayscaled, reduced opacity.

Page 7 (CC) – "Flower Garden Bokeh," by Torsten Behrens (Flickr) – cropped, grayscaled, reduced opacity.

Page 10 (CC) – "Garden flowers," by Nathan Cooprider (Flickr) – cropped, grayscaled, reduced opacity.

Page 11 (CC) – Dandelions, Robert Engelhardt – cropped, grayscaled, reduced opacity.

Page 21 – "Students at High Shoals elementary plant for the second time with the help of Dean Angle and Representative Chuck Williams," reprinted with permission from April Sorrow/University of Georgia College of Agricultural and Environmental Sciences – cropped, grayscaled.

Page 22 (CC) – "Garden," by Derek Bridges (Flickr) – cropped, grayscaled.

Page 23 (CC) – "Blood-red aphids," by Benny Mazur (Flickr) – cropped, grayscaled, reduced opacity.

Page 25 (CC) – "Garden tools," by Spitfire (Wikimedia Commons) – cropped, grayscaled, reduced opacity.

Page 34 (CC) – "Garden storage shed," by Gayle Easterly (Flickr) – grayscaled.

Page 38 (CC) – "NAUGHTY! (but omg look at that face)," by Karen (Flickr) – grayscaled.

Page 41 (CC) – "Pair of old leather gardening gloves," by Gratuit– cropped, grayscaled, background removed.

Page 47 — "Bags of soil at Haggen," reprinted with permission from Kevyn Jacobs (Flickr).

Page 49 (CC) – "Common dandelions," by Kreuzschnabel (Wikimedia Commons) – cropped, grayscaled, reduced opacity.

Page 51 (CC) – "Cabbage 2," by J.E. Theriot (Flickr) – cropped, grayscaled.

Page 56 (CC) – "Strawberries and Cream, Empress Hotel," by Robin Zebrowski (Flickr) – cropped, grayscaled.

Page 57 (CC) — "Grazing aphids," by Martin Cooper (Flickr) – grayscaled.

Page 58 — Shovel, by Goumbik (Pixabay) – cropped, grayscaled.

Page 62 (CC) – "Another plant goes in," U.S. Fish and Wildlife Service Southeast Region (Flickr) — cropped, grayscaled, reduced opacity.

Page 66 (CC) – "Dandelions," by Cristian V (Flickr) – cropped, grayscaled, reduced opacity.

Page 69 (CC) – "Garden hose, resting," by marysalome (Flickr) – grayscaled.

Page 70 (CC) – "Dandelions," by David J (Flickr) – cropped, grayscaled.

Page 75 (CC) – "Weeds," by Tony Alter (Flickr) – cropped, grayscaled.

Page 76 (CC) – "Dandelions," by Mike Mozart (Flickr) – cropped, grayscaled.

Page 78 (CC) – "Rose," by Susanne Nilsson (Flickr) – cropped, grayscaled.

Page 79 – "Rainbow Dawn" (dandelion in sidewalk), reprinted with permission from Anders Sandberg (Flickr) – grayscaled.

Page 81 (CC) — "Papa turned 95 today," by Carol VanHook – cropped, grayscaled.

Page 82 – "Campsis24," by Angelo Brathot (Flickr) – cropped, grayscaled, reduced opacity.

Page 84 (CC) – "Nezara viridula on a leaf," by Stanze (Flickre) – cropped, grayscaled.

Page 86 (CC) – "Rose," by al3lilo (Flickr) – cropped, grayscaled.

Page 87 (CC) – Garden hose (Smith College Plant Houses and Gardens, Northampton MA), Rusty Clark (Flickr) – cropped, grayscaled.

Page 90 (CC) — "Grasshopper," by Cuatrok77 (Flickr) — cropped, grayscaled, reduced opacity.

Page 91 (CC) – "Praying Mantis," by Patrick Kavanaugh (Flickr) – cropped.

Page 92 (CC) — "Beetle porn," by Christian Gloor (Flickr) — cropped, grayscaled, reduced opacity.

Page 94 (CC) — "Butterfly sex," by John Samuel (Flickr) – grayscaled.

Page 95 (CC) – "Dutch Nursery," by Bert Knottenbeld (Flickr) – cropped, grayscaled.

Page 96 (CC) – "Snail-orama, crossing the road," by JP (Fllickr) – grayscaled.

Page 97 — "Part of Almondsbury Garden Centre, near Bristol, England," by Adrian Pingstone (cropped, grayscaled, reduced opacity).

Page 108 (CC) – "Goldfinch," by stanze (Flickr) – cropped, grayscaled, rotated horizontally.

Page 108 (CC) – "Day 123: A Pile of Dirt to Call Our Own," by Quinn Dombrowski (Flickr) – cropped, grayscaled.

Page 112 (CC) – "Formal gardens," by Wendy (Flickr) – cropped, grayscaled.

Page 114 – "Yesterday's garden," reprinted with permission from by Zoë (Flickr).

Page 128 (CC) – "Malagos Garden Resort, Davao," by Thrifty Look (Flickr) – cropped, grayscaled.

Page 130 – "Blooming period," by Angelo Brathot (Flickr) – cropped, grayscaled, reduced opacity.

Page 134 – "Strange Flower," reprinted with permission from Stanley Zimny (Flickr – flickr.com/photos/stanzim/) – cropped, grayscaled.

Page 136 (CC) – Woman in tomato garden, by US Department of Agriculture (Flickr) – cropped, grayscaled.

Page 144 (CC) – "Squirrels," by James Havard (Flickr) – cropped, grayscaled, reduced opacity.

Page 146 – "Rusty wheelbarrow," by SuKaduna (Pixabay) – grayscaled.

Page 148 – "Large earthworm in the palm of a person's hand," by Ivan Radic (Flickr) – cropped, grayscaled, reduced opacity.

Page 151 – "Cow Pie," by Larry Koester, Mandrogy Collective, Russia (Flickr) – cropped, grayscaled.

Page 152 (CC) – Herb garden, by Green Mountain Girls Farm (Flickr) – cropped, grayscaled, reduced opacity.

Page 157 (CC) – "Earthworms!" by Chief G_G (Flickr) – cropped, grayscaled, reduced opacity.

Page 164 (CC) – "Garden Gnome Girl," by Chris Combe (Flickr) – cropped, grayscaled, reduced opacity.

Page 166 (CC) – "Above view of young girl planting seedlings in the garden," by Nenad Stojkovic (Flickr) – grayscaled.

Page 168 (CC) – "Enormous dusky eggplant, average sized boy — harvesting the eggplant that time forgot," by Woodleywonderworks (Flickr) – cropped, grayscaled.

Page 169 – "Liah Montgomery (3) helps pick and deliver a watermelon for the USDA's Veg U. . . . ", U.S. Department of Agriculture (Flickr) – cropped, grayscaled.

Page 170 (CC) – "Girl picks rose buds in Bishoftu, Ethiopia," by International Potash Institute Switzerland (Flickr) – cropped, grayscaled.

Page 171 (CC) – Caterpillar on leaf, by Goatling (Flickr) — cropped, grayscaled.

Page 172 (CC) – "Polygonia interrogationis, Occoquan Bay National Wildlife Refuge, Woodbridge, Virginia," by Judy Gallagher (Flickr) – grayscaled.

Page 174 (CC) – "Lily," by Richard Stubbs (Flickr) – cropped, grayscaled, reduced opacity.

Page 178 (CC) – "Stripey Green Grub 2," by Doug Beckers — cropped, grayscaled.

Page 180 – "Purdue Horticulture Gardens 07-28-2017 3," reprinted with permission from David Ellis (Flickr).

Page 183 (CC) – "As My Garden Grows," by Alan Levine, public domain.

Page 184 (CC) – "Lawn Mower," by Rafael Castillo (Flickr) – cropped, grayscaled, reduced opacity.

Page 186 (CC) – "Must mow the lawn," by Mat Wal (Flickr) – grayscaled.

Page 187 (CC) – "Hannah in the tall grass," by Amber Strocel (Flickr) – cropped, grayscaled.

Page 190 – "Elephant ear plant (Colocasia) in Louisiana," by Eric Svendson.

Page 193 – "Squash bug, Coreus marginatus," by Noel Feans (Wikimedia Commons) – grayscaled.

Page 194 (CC) – "I just finished mowing the lawn," by Q Family (Flickr) – grayscaled.

Page 196 (CC) – "Helping dad mow the Lawn," by EAndrew Dawes (Flickr) – cropped, grayscaled, reduced opacity.

Page 198 – "Making the hay: Life of 2006 in the countryside of northern Portugal," by Hanna Norlin (Flickr) – grayscaled.

Page 201 – "Dock bug," by Stanze (Flickr) – cropped, grayscaled, reduced opacity.

Page 204 (CC) – "Lunchtime," by Nishanth Jois (Flickr) – cropped, grayscaled.

Page 205 (CC) – "Where's the afterparty?" (Original title: "Leaves with chewing damage at Kipahulu camp Haleakala National Park, Maui, Hawaii"), by Forest and Kim Starr (Flickr) – grayscaled.

Page 207 (CC) — "Looks like I'll need a rope," by Dennis Loveridge.

Page 208 (CC) — "Dirty dog," by Christian Gauthier (Flickr) – cropped, grayscaled.

Page 209 (CC) – Woman in t-shirt, by Spread Group – grayscaled, artwork added.

Page 210 (CC) — "Potted plants," by Lorna Mitchell (Flickr) — cropped, grayscaled, reduced opacity.

Page 213 (CC) — Garden shop, by Franklin Heijnen (Flickr) – cropped, grayscaled.

Page 215 (CC) – "If you can't pot them, boot them" (original title: "Christianian Iorontziak"), by Eider Palmou (Flicker) – grayscaled.

Page 217 (CC) – “Raised bed vegetable garden,” by Normanack (Flickr) – cropped, grayscaled, reduced transparency.

Page 224 (CC) – “Lycosidae – licósidos ‘araña lobo’” (Lycosidae lichens “wolf spider”), by Jacinta lluch Valero (Flickr) – cropped, grayscaled, reduced opacity.

Page 229 (CC) – Cutworm, Clemson University - USDA Cooperative Extension Slide Series, Bugwood.org – cropped, grayscaled.

Page 231 (CC) — “Vegetable garden, herb garden on the Kirchberg plateau, Reinhausen (Gleichen),” by Nemracc (Wikimedia Commons) — cropped, grayscaled, person in hazmat suit added.

Page 233 (CC) – “Compost,” by Alachua County (Flickr) – Oregon State University's student-run organic farm in Corvallis – grayscaled.

Page 235 – “Sphagnum,” reprinted with permission from Ben Zvan Photography.

Page 239 – “*Cucurbita pepo subsp. pepo Zucchini* (zucchini) at Bichlhäusl in Frankenfels, Austria,” by GT1976 (Wikimedia Commons) – cropped, grayscaled, reduced opacity.

Page 245 (CC) – “Zucchini,” by Jeremy Keith (Flickr) – grayscaled.

Page 247 (CC) – “Take my zucchini,” US Department of Agriculture, Institute of American Indian Arts, Land-Grant Tribal College and University Land-Grant program (Gardner: Teresa Kaulaity Quintana, Kiowa) – cropped, grayscaled.

Page 248 (CC) – “Datura stramonium (Jimson weed), Leaves chewed with 3 lined potato beetle adults at Kawela Bridge, Molokai, Hawaii,” by Forest and Kim Starr (Flickr) – cropped, grayscaled, rotated horizontally, reduced opacity.

Page 250 (CC) – “Two Jewels,” by Rison Thumboor (Flickr) – cropped, grayscaled.

Page 254 (CC) – “Praying mantis,” by Ted (Flickr) – grayscaled.

Page 255 (CC) – “Echeveria Elegans, Echeveria Anemone, Pachyphytum Compactum, Sedeveria Letizia,” by Stephen Boisvert (Flickr) – cropped, grayscaled, reduced opacity.

Page 260 (CC) – “Crazy French Guy,” by miguelb (Flickr) – grayscaled.

Page 261 (CC) – “Two naughty kittens,” by Shellac (Flickr) – grayscaled.

Page 262 (CC) – "Commercial Street Toddler Planters," by b k (Flickr) – grayscaled.

Page 264 (CC) – "Old Swan House," by Herry Lawford (Flickr) – cropped, grayscaled, reduced opacity.

Page 268 (CC) – "Herb Garden," by Jack Ketcham (Flickr) – cropped, grayscaled, reduced opacity.

Page 271 (CC) — "Freaky carrot," by John Bointon (Flickr) — cropped, grayscaled, rotated, background removed.

Page 282 (CC) — "Mangoes," by Joegoauk Goa (Flickr) — cropped, grayscaled, reduced opacity.

Page 283 (CC) — "Mango," by ilf (Flickr) — cropped, grayscaled.

Page 271 (CC) – Strange carrot," by Bo&Ko (Flickr) – grayscaled, background removed.

Page 284 (CC) – "Anther of hibiscus," by Surajmondol (Wikimedia Commons) — cropped, grayscaled, reduced opacity, rotated.

Page 286 (CC) – Couple in garden, by Artur Potosi (Flickr), Russia – grayscaled.

Page 291 (CC) – "Sphagnum auriculatum," by Berndt Haynold (Creative Commons) – cropped, grayscaled.

Page 292 (CC) – Rabbit at attention, by Alan Sandercock (Flickr) – cropped, grayscaled, reduced opacity.

Page 296 (CC) – "Hoop hoop," by Akash UK (Flickr) – grayscaled.

Page 298 (CC) – "Red Mites (Balaustium sp.) on Convolvulus flower," Bernard Dupont (Flickr) – cropped, grayscaled, reduced opacity.

Page 299 (CC) – "Happy World Naked Gardening Day," by Miltof (Flickr) – grayscaled.

Page 300 (CC) – "Squashes," by Ruth Hartnup (Flickr) – cropped, grayscaled, reduced opacity.

Page 303 (CC) – "Meet my new friend kale," by Kate Ter Haar (Flickr) – cropped, grayscaled, reduced opacity.

Page 306 (CC) – "Students at High Shoals elementary plant for the second time with the help of Dean Angle," by April Sorrow – cropped, grayscaled, reduced opacity.

Page 308 (CC) – "Cabbage or repolho," by Under the same moon . . . (Flickr) – cropped, grayscaled.

Page 309 (CC) – "Carrots," by Jeff Egnaczyk (Flickr) – cropped, grayscaled, reduced opacity.

Page 311 – "Kindred carrots," reprinted with permission from Jane Pellicciotto (Flickr).

Page 313 — "Carrot Love," reprinted with permission from Tara Saberon, Evergreen Farm, Smoot, Wyoming.

Page 314 — "What the hell are they spraying on vegetables these days?" reprinted with permission from Rexaquionis (Reddit) — grayscaled.

Page 318 (CC) – "Vermont Ave Garden-Work Party, Washington, DC," by Ted Eytan (Flickr) – cropped, grayscaled, reduced opacity.

Page 319 (CC) — "Grasshopper," by Cuatrok77 (Flickr) — cropped, grayscaled, reduced opacity.

Page 320 (CC) – "Larval lepidopterans on buttonbush leaf, Newark, Ohio, USA," by James St. John – grayscaled.

Page 323 – "Broccoli harvest," reprinted with permission from Scott Sherrill-Mix (Flicker) – cropped, grayscaled.

Page 325 (CC) – "Garden," by Drew Folta (Flickr) – cropped, grayscaled, reduced opacity.

Page 330 – "Huellas de Acahualinca: 2,100-year-old human footprints preserved in volcanic mud near the lake in Managua, Nicaragua," by Dr. d12 (Wikimedia Commons) – cropped, grayscaled, reduced opacity.

Page 331 (CC) – "Ol Doinyo Lengai volcano near Lake Natro," by Richard Mortel (Flickr) – grayscaled.

Page 337 (CC) – "Pea aphid," by Andy Murray (Flickr) – cropped, grayscaled, reduced opacity.

Page 348 (CC) – "Mixed berry," by kkmarais (Flickr) – cropped, grayscaled, reduced opacity.

Page 350 (CC) – "Trowel," by Jag2020 (Pixabay) – cropped, grayscaled.

ALSO FROM QUIPPERY

And more Quippery books are on the way. If you'd like to be notified when they come out, go to Quippery.com and sign up on our email list, and we'll be sure to let you know.

Thanks for reading!

To order books – tinyurl.com/quippery

Quippery videos – The amazing messages hidden in the names of people and places — tinyurl.com/Quipperyvideos

Contact us – Quippery.com

GIVING BACK

We pledge to donate a percentage of our profits in support of planet and people, through the vital work of two nonprofit organizations:

Planet

Since 1951, **The Nature Conservancy** (nature.org) has worked to protect the lands and waters on which all life depends.

People

The **David Lynch Foundation** (davidlynchfoundation.org) supports the health, well-being, and personal development of at-risk students, veterans suffering from PTSD, women and girls who have been the victims of violence, people living with HIV/AIDS, prisoners, and at-risk children in other countries.

Quippery

Happy trowels to you
Till we meet again

Made in the USA
Monee, IL
14 December 2022